STANDING
ON THE
RocK

Also by James Montgomery Boice

Witness and Revelation in the Gospel of John
Philippians: An Expositional Commentary
The Sermon on the Mount
How to Live the Christian Life (originally, How to Live It Up)
Ordinary Men Called by God (originally, How God Can Use Nobodies)
The Last and Future World
The Gospel of John: An Expositional Commentary (5 volumes in one)
"Galatians" in the Expositor's Bible Commentary
Can You Run Away from God?
Our Sovereign God, editor
Our Savior God: Studies on Man, Christ and the Atonement, editor
Does Inerrancy Matter?
The Foundation of Biblical Authority, editor
Making God's Word Plain, editor
The Epistles of John
Genesis: An Expositional Commentary (3 volumes)
The Parables of Jesus
The Christ of Christmas
The Minor Prophets: An Expositional Commentary (2 volumes)
The Christ of the Open Tomb
Foundations of the Christian Faith (4 volumes in one)
Christ's Call to Discipleship
Transforming Our World: A Call to Action, editor
Ephesians: An Expositional Commentary
Daniel: An Expositional Commentary
Joshua: We Will Serve the Lord
Nehemiah: Learning to Lead
The King Has Come
Romans (3 volumes)
Mind Renewal in a Mindless Age
Amazing Grace

STANDING

ON THE

RocK

BIBLICAL AUTHORITY
IN A SECULAR AGE

JAMES MONTGOMERY BOICE

Baker Books

A Division of Baker Book House Co
Grand Rapids, Michigan 49516

Published by Baker Books
a division of Baker Book House Company
P.O. Box 6287, Grand Rapids, MI 49516-6287

Second printing, December 1994

Printed in the United States of America

Library of Congress Cataloging-in-Publication Data

Boice, James Montgomery, 1938–
    Standing on the rock : biblical authority in a secular age / by James
Montgomery Boice. — Rev. ed.
      p.   cm.
    Includes bibliographical references.
    ISBN 0-8010-1076-4
    1. Bible—Evidences, authority, etc. 2. Bible—Inspiration. I. Title.
BS480.B59   1994
220.1'3—dc20
                                 93-36780

To the Giver
of every good and perfect gift,
who does not change like shifting shadows

CONTENTS

PREFACE TO THE 1984 EDITION

I sometimes ask myself why so many in our day have abandoned the church's traditionally high view of the Bible's inspiration, particularly at the point of its inerrancy or infallibility. If the evidence from archaeology, linguistic studies, historical investigations, and greater analysis of the Word of God tends in the direction of the Bible's overall reliability, why do so many find a high view of the Bible impossible?

I think the answer is intimidation. A person in seminary or even in a liberal church situation is often told: You know, I wouldn't take a conservative stand like that if I were you, because if you do, a lot of doors are going to be closed to you. You are not going to have the opportunities you would otherwise have.

People who are not firm in the conviction that they are God's servants before they are men's, and that their future is in the Lord's hands, sometimes tend to back off and compromise when confronted by such warnings. Or if they do not compromise out of fear, they may respond to ridicule.

Another churchman may smile at them, saying, I know there are people who still believe that the Bible is God's Word. But, you know, not many people do—at least not the educated people, not the professors, not the people who have investigated these subjects thoroughly. As a result of such sophisticated ridicule, the person who wants to stand for the Bible as being the Word of God is made to look or feel foolish.

I want to counter this intimidation and say that the results of serious investigation prove the very opposite. Serious study tends to support the Bible's inerrancy, and the facts are in no way inconsistent with the Bible being the very Word of God.

If the Bible is not the unique revelation of God to fallen men and women, then there is no such revelation anywhere. And this is contrary to what we should expect, even on the basis of our knowledge of ourselves as human beings!

To begin with, we should know there is a God and that he must have made us, for nothing can come into existence by itself. Creation must have a Creator. God cannot have created things greater than himself, so everything we value about ourselves must have a larger and perfect expression in him. One of the things we most value about ourselves is our desire for and ability to communicate. To communicate with others is part of what it means to be a person. But if we desire and can communicate in our own limited ways, God (from whom this proper desire and great ability comes) must possess this desire and ability in fuller measure. We should, therefore, expect that God wants to communicate with us and has in fact done so. The questions should therefore be, not Has God spoken? but Where has God spoken? and What do we need to hear to be obedient to that revelation?

In this book I make the case that the Bible is this revelation of God, that receiving its testimony is necessary for our salvation and for the health of the church, that it is possible to answer the attacks of higher criticism on its own terms, and that sound principles of Bible study will enable anyone to understand the Bible and profit from it spiritually.

To study the history of human attacks upon the Bible is a reminder of the instability and error of all things human. Critics of a former generation are soon forgotten. But it is also a reminder of how, throughout this same period, the Bible has stood like a rock and has been a sure refuge for those who have built upon it.

PREFACE TO THE 1994 EDITION

It has been a full decade since the publication of *Standing on the Rock*, the book that contained the substance of the lectures I delivered across the country on behalf of the International Council on Biblical Inerrancy during the decade of its existence (from 1978–1988). ICBI was led by such outstanding evangelical leaders as Francis Schaeffer, J. I. Packer, A. Wetherell Johnson, R. C. Sproul, John Gerstner, Roger Nicole, and others. The Council's explicit purpose was the task of "elucidating, vindicating and applying the doctrine of biblical inerrancy as an essential element for the authority of Scripture and a necessity for the health of the church of God." The council voted to end its work in the fall of 1988 because the sixteen members of the council felt they had accomplished everything they could themselves accomplish in the area of biblical inerrancy and did not want merely to perpetuate another evangelical organization. ICBI had the distinction of being one of those exceedingly few organizations that have actually completed their work and disbanded.

But the issue of biblical authority remains, of course. It will always be a foundational matter for the church's health, hence the republishing of these lectures.

However, I have noticed something new since the final meeting of ICBI in the fall of 1988, and that is a subtle shift in the nature of the challenge confronting evangelicals. The International Council on Biblical Inerrancy did its work so well that few who

11

call themselves evangelicals today openly denigrate biblical authority or criticize the doctrine of inerrancy. It is "bad press" to do that. And dangerous! But there is a moving away from biblical authority all the same in the sense that increasing numbers no longer believe that the Bible is sufficient for the church to do its work. The Bible is often laid aside and reliance is placed instead upon such extra-biblical props as sociological techniques, psychology and psychiatry, and what are called "signs and wonders."

In some cases there is some value in these things—a sociological study of one's community, for instance, so one can reach it better, or psychiatric help for a person who is seriously maladjusted or disturbed. But what has troubled me is the increasing tendency to turn to such techniques rather than to the Bible even to the point of neglecting the Word of God completely.

Moreover, in the case of what are called "signs and wonders," I am convinced that this is a serious and ultimately disastrous departure from the way in which God has told us to evangelize.

Because of this concern I have added a final, seventh chapter to the six original chapters of *Standing on the Rock*. It is an expanded, edited version of a message I gave to the Sunday morning congregation of Tenth Presbyterian Church of Philadelphia on the occasion of a celebration marking twenty-five years of ministry to Tenth and that city. The fact I chose this subject for such a significant occasion should signal the seriousness with which I regard this matter. As for the other chapters in this book, they have been edited slightly to update them, but they are essentially what appeared in the original 1984 edition.

As I move into the last decades of my preaching and teaching ministry, I am reminded of what Jesus said about the Bible. He said, "Heaven and earth will pass away, but my words will never pass away" (Matt. 24:35). I have seen many human theories and many popular fads come and go. But the Word of God remains like a rock in the midst of raging storms, treacherous offshore currents, and nearly invisible quicksands. It is good it does, because only the one who builds on this rock will truly stand forever.

1

A PLACE TO STAND

When I was chairman of the International Council on Biblical Inerrancy, I was frequently asked whether one's particular view of the Bible matters all that much. Sometimes the question was asked by people who were merely preoccupied with a personal relationship with Jesus Christ.

Why does a particular view of the Bible matter so long as we have faith in Christ? they said. Doesn't a preoccupation with the Bible detract from our relationship to Christ?

Other people were concerned with biblical inerrancy because they consider the doctrine to be wrong. They said, Inerrancy gets us caught up in the trivia of Scripture and makes us forget about the Bible's great themes. Isn't it enough to have just a general knowledge of Scripture and a basic faith in its integrity?

The views of many of these people would be: The Holy Spirit still works through the Bible. People are still saved. Defense of the Bible does not require the kind of effort being made today by many who affirm its full authority and defend it as being without error in the whole and in its parts.

In 1979, shortly after the International Council on Biblical Inerrancy was organized, I received an invitation from a group of students at Princeton Theological Seminary to come to that campus to present what ICBI was about. Since I had attended the seminary some years before, I knew that the school was not likely to be friendly to this doctrine. I could imagine a situation in which I would be confronted by a team of professors asking me about the latest scholarly article denying a high view of biblical inspiration, which I, of course, would not even have read.

I took the safe way out and asked someone to go with me: Dr. John H. Gerstner, a member of the Inerrancy Council and, at the time a professor at Princeton's sister institution, Pittsburgh Theological Seminary. The day arrived, and the two of us appeared on campus.

I was surprised by two things. First, I had expected perhaps twenty students to be interested in a lecture on the Bible (plus the team of hostile professors). But instead there were between three and four hundred students in the room—and no professors. Obviously inerrancy was a matter of keen interest among the student body.

The second surprise was this. We were to eat together from 12:00 noon to 12:30 P.M. I was to lecture from 12:30 to 1:15. Then we were to answer questions until 1:30. But when 1:30 came nobody left. The students did not leave at 2:30 either, or at 3:30. At 4:00, Dr. Gerstner and I were still there trying to explain why a sure word from God is essential for our own salvation and for having a message for the world.

I did not think we had made much progress, because most of the students had a most subjective faith, based on their feelings. They did not see the need for anything else. But the following week, after Dr. Gerstner and I had returned home, I received a letter from one student which is worth quoting.

> I have never held to the doctrine of inerrancy, and yet I found myself siding with you as today's discussion proceeded. Is it not true that behind most of the questions you received was a crypto-cultural Christianity, that is, a secret capitulation to the try-it-you'll-like-it mentality of our civilization? That is how it seemed to me. Most questioners did not seem to be engaged in a point-for-point argument over any substantial theological issue. Rather, most seemed to think that to preach the gospel in this day and age, one doesn't need a place to stand. All that one has to do is stand in the pulpit and say, not Thus saith the Lord, but only Try it, you'll like it.
>
> I am surprised that I found myself feeling that you were right and all of us were wrong, at least insofar as this very basic point is concerned: Why we stand where we stand makes all the difference in the world.

What kind of a difference does it make? It makes a difference in three areas: for us individually as Christians, for preaching, and for the health of the church.

A Place for Me

We live in a relativistic age in which many people do not have a firm view of truth and are therefore adrift so far as any intellectual moorings are concerned. Most of the great apologists of our time have said the same thing in one form or another.

I remember the first time I came across the idea that there is no firm view of truth today. It was in college when I first read C. S. Lewis's *The Screwtape Letters*. Wormwood, the junior devil, had written to Screwtape, his superior, to get advice on how he should handle his "patient," a man who was about to become a Christian. Wormwood had introduced him to a materialist who had been giving him reasons why he should not believe in Christianity. This plan had not worked very well. By presenting his arguments the materialist had caused the patient to think, and as he thought, some of the evidences for Christianity had begun to get through to him. Wormwood wanted to know what he should do. In the first letter Screwtape replied that a rationalistic approach to the patient was wrong, because today people do not operate on the basis of arguments. He said that the way to deal with the patient was not to convince him that Christianity was wrong, but that it was outworn, academic, or irrelevant. "Jargon, not argument, is your best ally in keeping him from the Church," wrote Screwtape.[1]

After this I read works by Francis Schaeffer, who develops this idea in a fuller way. He traces the root of the problem to the view of truth held by Georg Wilhelm Friedrich Hegel. Hegel is the thinker who developed the idea of the "historical dialectic," which means that there is always struggle in history and that history proceeds through struggle and resolution.

Hegel believed that in any period of history there is a dominant idea, which he called a *thesis*. This dominant idea will rule for a time. People will accept it as true, but eventually it will produce a reaction. People will see its limitations and develop an alternative to it. He called this alternative an *antithesis*. Then history enters a period in which the thesis, on the one side, and the antithesis, on the other side, struggle with each other. For a while nobody knows where to stand. But eventually, as these two struggle within the historical process, there comes about a merging or *synthesis*. Parts of each get dropped off. Other points are strengthened and changed. For a time everything seems to come back together again. This synthesis becomes the new thesis. But because there are no absolutes in history, the thesis eventually produces a new reaction, which becomes a new antithesis, which in turn gives way to a new synthesis, and so on. All of history is like that, according to Hegel.

This view suggests that something may be considered true in one period of history, say, in the latter decades of the twentieth century, where we stand now. But it will be true only so far as we ourselves are concerned. It may not be true in the year 2000. Again, although it is true for us, it is not necessarily true for other people. There are no absolutes. Whether they recognize it or not, this is the philosophical basis on which most people are operating in our time.

We can see this clearly by watching what happens when we try to witness in an informal way, when we are sitting down one-to-one with another person sharing Christ. We talk about Jesus as the Son of God, the Savior, who died for our sin, rose from the dead, and is coming again. What happens? A generation ago when a Christian would do that with one who did not believe or who did not want to believe, he generally got an argument. The person who did not like what he was saying would explain why most people could not believe it: There is no such thing as a resurrection. Resurrections do not happen. Miracles do not occur. This is the scientific age. We know that once a person is dead he is always dead, he would argue.

But what happens when we present the claims of Christ today? Sometimes we meet a particularly argumentative person, somebody who has been reading the old liberal literature and wants to defend these ideas. He might argue. But, generally speaking, we do not get arguments today. Usually people will say, I am glad you have found something meaningful for you, but that is just not my bag. What they mean is that it is truth for you, but it is not truth for me; I have a different kind of truth in my own area.

When people operate on that basis, they usually think they have found freedom because, in not being tied to absolutes, they have freedom to do anything they wish. They are not tied to God or to a God-given morality. They do not have to acknowledge any authority. But the consequence of this kind of freedom is that they are cast adrift on the sea of meaningless existence.

If there are no absolutes—no final truth as to where we are coming from, who has made us, what we are doing here, or what lies ahead—then ultimately our existence here has no meaning. If there are no absolutes, there are no absolutes for us. We are here, and that is fine. We will die, and that is also fine. Nobody will be the poorer for our loss.

We see this truth expressed in the realm of words. If there are no absolutes, then words or what they stand for are not absolutes either, so ultimately words are meaningless. Some years ago there was a seminary class in which one of the professors was expounding a relativistic view of truth. He was insisting that language has no absolute meaning. "It means what it means to you, but what it means to you is not necessarily what it means to me." He said that we can never communicate in any absolute sense.

The students were arguing with the professor because, to their "untutored" minds, this did not seem to make sense. One said, "That is not right! It is true that sometimes language is ambiguous. That is why we write dictionaries and word books to explain what we mean. That is why we teach and argue points. We go back and forth to try to understand where the other person is coming from. But it is not true that language is always ambiguous, and the less ambiguous it is, the better." Another continued, "For example, if you look out the window and see an airplane in the sky and say, 'Look, an airplane!' everybody looks up. Why do they do that? It is because the word 'airplane' carries some objective content. It is not an empty term."

The professor did not agree. He kept pressing his point. So, finally, one of the students said, "You know, if language is meaningless, then the language we are speaking here is meaningless. And if the language we are speaking here is meaningless, our being here is meaningless." He waited until that sank in.

Then another student asked, "Well, if this is meaningless, what are we going to do with the rest of the hour?"

A third student said, "Let's play squash." So the class got up, went out the door, and left the professor alone in the classroom with his theory.

That same illustration can be applied to the churches. If we do not have a sure word from God with objective content, then what we are doing in our churches is as meaningless as what that professor was doing in his classroom. If that is true, the most rational thing a congregation can do is get up and walk out. This is just what congregations are doing in many liberal churches. They are showing with their feet that modern theology has no meaning.

You need a place to stand as a Christian, and you have it in the Bible. The Bible speaks in absolute terms: "Thus says the Lord." In these terms the Bible teaches about God, who brought everything into existence; about ourselves as his creatures—who we are, what we have become, and what we can be; about Jesus Christ as the only way of salvation; about a hell to be avoided and a heaven to be won.

Arthur Schopenhauer, the German pessimistic philosopher, did not always dress well and sometimes, it was said, appeared quite unkempt. On one occasion he was in a park in Berlin when a policeman came by and, thinking he was a derelict, said to Schopenhauer, "Who do you think you are?"

Schopenhauer replied, "I would to God I knew."

The only way Schopenhauer, or any of us, can find out who we are is from God in Scripture, and the only way we can become what he would have us be is by building on the truths of salvation that are found there.

A Place for Preaching

The Bible also gives preachers a place to stand. Relativism is a difficult problem for individuals today. But the difficulty with preaching is that many preachers no longer really believe that the Bible is the Word of God. They believe it to be the words of mere men, fallible men. They can no longer say, "Thus saith the Lord," but instead "It seems to me. . . . "

For a long time I moved in rather liberal church circles and often spoke to liberal congregations. I found that lay people particularly do not know how bad the situation is. Some denominations have a high view of Scripture, and some individual preachers have a high view of Scripture but, by and large, the majority of preachers across America today do not hold to that high view historically held by the church.

Generally, pastors do not talk much about this. If they did, some would lose their jobs. Although they are not open with their parishioners, they are often quite outspoken in gatherings of other ministers.

A number of years ago I took part in a series of meetings called Moderator's Conferences, sponsored by the moderator of the United Presbyterian Church. A variety of people came: leading pastors, seminary professors, and denominational staff. I presented a paper on "The Mission of the Church as Evangelism," speaking about the lost condition of people apart from the gospel, and about Jesus' work in history to achieve our salvation. When I was finished there were question-and-answer periods. On one occasion a professor from one of the leading theological seminaries objected to almost everything I had said. He did not like my emphasis on the lostness of men and women. Neither did he like my reference to the historical Jesus, nor my understanding of the gospel.

At one point he said, "There is no such thing as the historical Jesus!" Looking in my direction he continued, "Don't you know that each of the Gospels was written to contradict the other Gospels?"

No, as a matter of fact, I did not know that. I thought they were complementary.

Then, because I had said something about Jesus coming again, he added, "We have got to get it into our heads that Jesus is never coming back. All things are going to continue as they have from the beginning."

That did not surprise me, because the professor was inadvertently quoting 2 Peter 3:3–4: "First of all, you must understand that in the last days scoffers will come, scoffing and following their own evil desires. They will say, 'Where is this "coming" he promised? Ever since our fathers died, everything goes on as it has since the beginning of creation.'" The only thing that did startle me was the openness with which a man in his position would utterly discount the Bible as the Word of God.

For many years a friend of mine worked in presbytery meetings to present an evangelical position and argue for evangelical concerns. On one occasion another minister asked, "Matthew, why are you always quoting the Bible when you stand up to argue a point? Don't you know that nobody believes the Bible anymore? Don't you know that the apostle Paul is not infallible?"

This sometimes occurs even in evangelical circles. In 1981, newspapers carried reports of an address given by Dr. Robert G. Bratcher during a three-day national seminar of the Southern Baptist Christian Life Commission. Bratcher had been a translator of the *Good News for Modern Man* Bible, which would suggest that he held to a high view of Scripture. But apparently he did not. He said in his address:

> Only willful ignorance or intellectual dishonesty can account for the claim that the Bible is inerrant and infallible. . . . No truth-loving, God-respecting, Christ-honoring believer should be guilty of such heresy. To invest the Bible with the qualities of inerrancy and infallibility is to idolatrize it, to transform it into a false God. . . .
>
> Often in the past, and still too often in the present, to affirm that the Bible is the Word of God implies that the words of the Bible are the words of God. Such simplistic and absolute terms divest the Bible altogether of its humanity and remove it from the relativism of the historical process. No one seriously claims that all the words of the Bible are the very words of God. . . . Quoting what the Bible says in the context of history and culture is not necessarily relevant or helpful—and may be a hindrance in trying to meet and solve the problems we face. . . .
>
> Even words spoken by Jesus in Aramaic in the thirties of the first century and preserved in writing in Greek thirty-five to fifty years later do not necessarily wield compelling or authentic authority over us today.[2]

These are harsh words. Bratcher is not merely saying that the words of the Bible may misrepresent the teachings of Jesus and therefore do not have authority over us today, but that the actual words of Jesus do not have authority over us today. In other words, Jesus does not have authority! No wonder this unbelieving professor says at the end of his address, "It is the height of presumption and arrogance to say, 'I know this is God's will, and I am doing it.'"

These statements represent an abnormal situation. In the past everyone in the church believed that the Bible was the Word of God. Even the heretics believed it. They held to bad theology, but they at least got it (wrongly) out of the Bible. Their errors required the church to come together to analyze the Scripture corporately and point out that the heretics were wrong. But even the heretics regarded the Scriptures as authoritative. The ancients reasoned that if the Bible is the Word of God, as it claims to be; and if God is a God of truth, as God must be; then the Bible must be true in the whole and in its parts. If it reports Jesus as saying that Moses wrote the Pentateuch (the first five books), then Moses wrote the Pentateuch. If 1 and 2 Timothy claim to be written by Paul, Paul wrote them. This kind of logic seems irrefutable if the Bible is the Word of God and if God is a God of truth.

Irenaeus, who lived and wrote in Lyons, France, in the early years of the second century, said that we should be "most properly assured that the Scriptures are indeed perfect, since they were spoken by the Word of God and his Spirit."[3]

Cyril of Jerusalem, who lived in the fourth century, argued, "Not even a casual statement must be delivered without the Holy Scriptures; nor must we be drawn aside by mere probability and artifices of speech. . . . For this salvation which we believe depends not on ingenious reasoning, but on demonstration of the Holy Scriptures."[4]

At the beginning of his treatise "On the Trinity," *Saint Augustine* wrote, "Do not be willing to yield to my writings as to the canonical Scriptures; but in these, when thou hast discovered even what thou didst not previously believe, believe it unhesitatingly."[5] Augustine said of the Scriptures, "I . . . believe most firmly that not one of those authors has erred in writing anything at all. If I do find anything in those books which seems contrary to truth, I decide that either the text is corrupt, or the translators did not follow what was really said, or that I failed to understand it. . . . The canonical books are entirely free of falsehood."[6]

Martin Luther wrote of the Old Testament, "I beg and faithfully warn every pious Christian not to be offended at the simplicity of the language and the stories that will often meet him here. Let him not doubt that, however simple they may seem, they are the very words, works, judgments, and deeds of the high majesty, power, and wisdom of God."[7] In another place the great Reformer said, "Scripture, although also written of men, is not of men nor from men, but from God."[8] In *Table Talk* he declared, "We must make a great difference between God's Word and the word of man. A man's word is a little sound that flies into the air, and soon vanishes; but the Word of God is greater than heaven and earth, yea, greater than death and hell, for it forms part of the power of God, and endures everlastingly."[9]

John Calvin, the Genevan Reformer, wrote similarly, "This is the principle that distinguishes our religion from all others, that we know that God has spoken to us and are fully convinced that the prophets did not speak of themselves, but, as organs of the Holy Spirit, uttered only that which they had been commissioned from heaven to declare. All those who wish to profit from the Scriptures must first accept this as a settled principle, that the Law and the prophets are not teachings handed on at the pleasure of men or produced by men's minds as their source, but are dictated by the Holy Spirit. . . . We owe to the Scripture the same reverence as we owe to God, since it has its only source in him and has nothing of human origin mixed with it."[10] In his comments on Psalm 5, Calvin speaks of the Bible as that "certain and unerring rule."

John Wesley said, "If there be any mistakes in the Bible, there may well be a thousand. If there be one falsehood in that book, it did not come from the God of truth."[11]

The same thing is true of more recent writers. *J. Gresham Machen* wrote that the Bible is "not partly true and partly false, but all true, the blessed, holy Word of God."[12]

R. A. Torrey declared, "The Bible is the Word of God. The voice that speaks to us from this book is the voice of God."[13]

Francis Schaeffer said, "The Bible is without mistake because it is God's inspired Word and . . . God cannot lie or contradict himself."[14]

J. I. Packer has written, "The only right attitude for us is to confess that our works are vile and our wisdom foolishness, and to receive with thankfulness the flawless righteousness and the perfect Scriptures which God in mercy gives us. Anything else is a conceited affront to divine grace. And evangelical theology is bound to oppose the attitude which undervalues the gift of Scripture and presumes to correct the inerrant Word of God."[15]

It is only when ministers of the gospel hold to this high view of Scripture that they can preach with authority and effectively call sinful men and women to full faith in Christ. If they do not have a sure word from God, they cannot preach a sure word from God. But if they do, even the most humbly endowed pastor will be effective.

A Place for My Church

Not only does the Bible give us a place to stand as lay Christians and as preachers, it gives us a place to stand as a church and makes the church healthy. Why? Because the Bible points to God and is the means by which God corrects the church's errors. If we do not know we have a sure word from God, or if we believe that the Bible is composed of truth mixed with error, what happens when we read a section of the Bible that calls on us to change? If we do not know we have an entirely truthful Bible, truthful down to the very words of the text, inerrant in the whole and in its parts, it will be that very part which calls for us to change that we will decide is in error. We will not want it to speak to us because we will not want to change. By this false view of Scripture, the role of the Bible as the reforming Word of God within the church is destroyed.

When the church takes its proper stand and teaches that the Bible is truthful, something else happens. Not only is sin disclosed, but individuals are also brought face to face with the God of Scripture. Despite the disturbing nature of that confrontation, it is what we need if we are to grow strong as God's children.

We do not have a strong church in America today, though numerically we may appear relatively strong. The Gallup Poll has identified forty or fifty million Americans as claiming to have had a born-again experience, and that is significant, even though all of these are probably not born again. Forty or fifty million is a large number of people. But strength does not come from numbers. Strength comes from quality of character, and what is most lacking in our churches is character formed by the knowledge of God. If God is not known as the sovereign, holy, omniscient, and unchangeable God the Bible declares him to be, then he cannot care for us, guide us or protect us. We cannot be strong in adverse circumstances.

The prophet Daniel had three friends, Shadrach, Meshach, and Abednego, who were confronted by Nebuchadnezzar's command to fall down and worship a great, golden statue. Many modern churchmen might, at that point, think of reasons why they should have obeyed Nebuchadnezzar. They might say, Look here, Shadrach, Meshach, and Abednego. We know that you are zealous young men. But young men sometimes lack the wisdom of their elders, and we would like to share a little bit of our wisdom with you. You have to think of everything that's involved. If you do not fall down and worship this statue, you are going to be killed. They are going to throw you into a burning, fiery furnace. You might be willing to have that happen, but think—that will be the end of your witness. You won't be any good to God dead.

If that did not work, they might argue theologically, saying, In the New Testament it is going to say "an idol is nothing." Now, if an idol is nothing, then to fall down and worship an idol is to fall down and worship nothing; and if nothing really is nothing, then your falling down can't possibly be construed as idolatry.

Or again, You have to understand that this isn't a question of worshiping a false God. Even Nebuchadnezzar does not believe that this idol is a god. This is just his symbol for the unity of the empire. It is like saluting the flag. That is all you have to do. Furthermore, Nebuchadnezzar likes you. I don't think you would even have to fall down on your face in the dirt. If you just stood in the back of the crowd and sort of tipped your head when the horn, flute, zither, lyre, harp, pipes, and all those other instruments sound, Nebuchadnezzar would say, I'll accept that as compliance. They mean well. Let them go.

Shadrach, Meshach, and Abednego did not buy that argument either, because they knew that God is God and that he was able to take care of them regardless of the circumstances. They replied to Nebuchadnezzar, "O Nebuchadnezzar, we do not need to defend ourselves before you in this matter. If we are thrown into the blazing furnace, the God we serve is able to save us from it, and he will rescue us from your hand, O king. But even if he does not, we want you to know, O king, that we will not serve your gods or worship the image of gold you have set up" (Dan. 3:16–18).

The world is setting up many false images. They are all around us. The ones who have strength not to bow down are those who know God from their study of the Scriptures.

J. C. Ryle, a bishop of the Church of England, said on one occasion: "Give me the plenary, verbal theory of biblical inspiration with all its difficulties, rather than the doubt. I accept the difficulties and I humbly wait for their solution. But while I wait, I am standing on rock."

2

THE WAY GOD SPEAKS

In the fall of 1980 I was in northern California for a seminar on "The Authority of Scripture" sponsored by the International Council on Biblical Inerrancy. Early in the morning, before the meetings were to start, I turned on the radio and heard a program the likes of which I had never heard before. It was a call-in show, which began with church bells. It was called "Have You Had a Spiritual Experience?"

While I listened, two callers told their stories. The first was a girl who explained how she had felt a sudden urge to leave her home in the northern part of the state and hitchhike down the coastal road. Halfway to Los Angeles she sensed that "this was the place." So she had the driver stop the car, got out, and went down the hill to the shore where she found a cave and camped out for a couple days. Then—because she thought God (or something) was leading her to do this—she went down into the water and mingled with the rocks and seaweed as if she were at the dawn of creation. Finally an animal came by, and she took this as a sign that it was time to go. She climbed the bank and hitchhiked back to northern California. That was her "spiritual experience."

The other person I listened to seemed to be an older woman. She said she had her experience quite recently—on Election Day. Jimmy Carter and Ronald Reagan were running in that election. She said, "I have always been a Democrat, and when I went into that voting booth I was planning to vote for Jimmy Carter. But something happened. A strange feeling came over me and I pulled the lever for Reagan." She did not say whether the influence she had felt was benign or demonic, but I think she believed it was the latter.

Is this the way God speaks to people? By feelings? Intuition? Strange, uncontrollable forces? Does God's Spirit lead us apart from the objective standard of his written word?

Word and Spirit

The Protestant Reformers gave a great deal of thought to this area, and their answer was always to stress the unity of the Word of God (the Bible) on the one hand, and the work of God's Holy Spirit illuminating the Word of God on the other. They said that you never have any true leading of God without both working together.

These men—Luther, Calvin, and others—had a very strong faith in the work of the Holy Spirit to teach and lead us. They believed this because they knew the Bible taught it. They thought of such verses as John 3:8: "The wind blows wherever it pleases. You hear its sound, but you cannot tell where it comes from or where it is going. So it is with everyone born of the Spirit." Or 1 John 5:6: "The Spirit . . . testifies, because the Spirit is the truth." Or 1 Corinthians 2:12–14: "We have not received the spirit of the world but the Spirit who is from God, that we may understand what God has freely given us. This is what we speak, not in words taught us by human wisdom but in words taught by the Spirit, expressing spiritual truths in spiritual words. The man without the Spirit does not accept the things that come from the Spirit of God, for they are foolishness to him, and he cannot understand them, because they are spiritually discerned."

But when they thought of these verses and others which stress the work of the Holy Spirit, Luther, Calvin, and the others also remembered other verses that taught the importance of the Bible in knowing the mind and will of God. They recognized that God speaks through the written Word.

Without the Holy Spirit the Bible is a dead book. That is why the man "without the Spirit" cannot understand it. On the other hand, without the Word as an objective guide from God, claims to a special leading by the Holy Spirit lead to error, excess, or the kind of foolishness heard on the "Have You Had a Spiritual Experience?" program.

I like what Martin Luther said. One day at the height of the Reformation, Luther was asked to write his name on the flyleaf of a copy of the German Bible he had translated. Luther did, but he wrote a message as well, beginning with John 8:25: "Who are you? . . . Even what I have told you from the beginning." Luther then added:

> They . . . desire to know who he is and not to regard what he says, while he desires them first to listen; then they will know who he is. The rule is: Listen and allow the Word to make the beginning; then the knowing will nicely follow. If, however, you do not listen, you will never know anything. For it is decreed: God will not be seen, known or comprehended except through his Word alone. Whatever, therefore, one undertakes for salvation apart from the Word is in vain. God will not respond to

that. He will not have it. He will not tolerate any other way.
Therefore, let his Book, in which he speaks with you, be com-
mended to you; for he did not cause it to be written for no purpose. He did not want us to let it lie there in neglect, as if he
were speaking with mice under the bench or with flies on the
pulpit. We are to read it, to think and speak about it, and to study
it, certain that he himself (not an angel or a creature) is speaking with us in it.[1]

Unfortunately, we often find ourselves getting off the track
in this area. Have you ever had the experience of being in doubt
about something you should do—having a decision to make and
not knowing how to make it—and finding yourself thinking or
perhaps even saying, Oh, if God would only speak to me directly!
If I could only hear a voice from heaven! If only an angel would
materialize in the room and give me a message from the Lord!
If God would only rearrange the stars of heaven to spell out a
message for me! Then I would know what God wants, come out
of my depression, and begin to go forward again. Have you ever
found yourself thinking along those lines? I know I have. Yet we
are far from God's thoughts when we reason this way.

In 2 Peter 1, where Peter spoke about his special experiences
as an apostle, he described the things he had that we do not
have. He listed them beginning, "we were eyewitnesses of his
majesty" (v. 16), that is to say, Our eyes actually saw Jesus Christ;
and furthermore we did not only see Christ in the flesh, where
his godhead was veiled, as it were, but rather in the moment of
his transfiguration. He appeared before us clothed in light. And
not only did we have this vision. We also heard a voice from
heaven, and the voice from heaven said clearly (we heard it with
our ears), "This is my Son, whom I love; with him I am well
pleased" (v. 17).

We read Peter's words and respond, Ah, yes, that is what we
want. We want that vision. We want that voice from heaven.
But how did Peter wrap this section up? Peter said, Ah, yes, but
what we have today is a more sure word, "the word of the

prophets made more certain," to which "you do well to pay attention . . . as to a light shining in a dark place" (v. 19).

Peter, who experienced the very thing we sometimes think we would like to have, said that his was an uncertain experience. It was not unimportant because he spoke as an eyewitness of Christ's majesty, and it was important that the apostles be eyewitnesses. But he said, If you want something that is really certain, don't desire a special, personal revelation from heaven but desire the Word of God, which is like a light shining in a dark place.

The important thing is the Word of God and how God reveals himself to us scripturally.

Two Kinds of Revelation

Revelation is a fairly broad word. One of the first things we notice is that the Bible teaches two different kinds of revelation. There is revelation in nature, which is usually called *general* revelation, and there is revelation in Scripture, which is usually called *specific* revelation.

General revelation refers to what we can know of God through nature. In the Old Testament the classic passage dealing with this subject is Psalm 19. This psalm falls into two parts. The first talks about nature and begins, "The heavens declare the glory of God; the skies proclaim the work of his hands" (v. 1). Whether you look up to the stars or whether you look down to the earth, there is a sense in which the entire creation shouts, "God!" The classic New Testament passage on this subject is Romans 1:18–20: "The wrath of God is being revealed from heaven against all the godlessness and wickedness of men who suppress the truth by their wickedness, since what may be known about God is plain to them, because God has made it plain to them. For since the creation of the world God's invisible qualities—his eternal power and divine nature—have been clearly seen, being understood from what has been made, so that men are without excuse."

In unqualified language these verses say that God has revealed certain things about himself in nature. These are important things, sufficient to direct men and women to God and therefore also sufficient to condemn them for their failure to seek out God. But this is a very limited revelation in that it does not teach us about the cross of Jesus Christ, the Christian life, the coming of the Holy Spirit, the church, or many other important doctrines. All it teaches is that God exists and that he is all-powerful. If I could put the two phrases "eternal power" and "divine nature" from Romans 1 into more philosophical language, I would say that God has shown in nature the existence of a Supreme (eternal power) Being (divine nature). That is, God exists. The evidence is plain. Men and women are guilty because they fail to seek him out as the true God.

When we say that God has revealed himself in nature and that men and women have nevertheless not sought him on the basis of that revelation, the question immediately arises, Why have men and women not done this? This is a fascinating question, because the reason is not that God cannot be known.

If you have ever attended a secular school and taken a course that gets into religious areas, you know how professors talk about God. For the most part they tend to dismiss the idea of God entirely. If they don't, if they really are liberally minded professors who do not want to eliminate any possibility without due argument and discussion, they will admit to the "possibility" of God and even speak of "the God-hypothesis." This statement does not mean that they believe in God. They probably think that no one in his right mind, if he truly investigates the possibility, would believe such an idea. But, nevertheless, God is at least a possibility—far out, it is true, far out on the fringes of thought, but nevertheless a possibility.

Paul says that this kind of thinking is dishonest. Nature does not merely admit the God-hypothesis, it forcefully and conclusively proclaims God's existence. So no one—not a child, not a scientist, not an American, not a European—has any excuse for failing to seek God out. God has made himself so clear in nature—so clear in a snowflake, a fingerprint, a grain of sand, a star, a quasar, anything you can think of—that all persons who do not seek him out on the basis of his general revelation are foolish and rebellious.

Why don't we seek him? Obviously, the problem is not intellectual. It is moral. We do not seek God out, not because God cannot be found or because the evidence does not point to him, but because we do not like the God who is to be found. He is an offense to us, and therefore we run away from him and suppress the truth. Why is the wrath of God revealed against men and women? Because they "suppress the truth" concerning him (v. 18). In other words, the truth of God is like a big spring. It threatens to leap up, change our lifestyle, and alter the way we think. It is because we do not want it to do this that we hold it down.

General revelation is ineffective so far as communication from God is concerned. It is not ineffective from the point of view of God's reason for giving it. General revelation exposes the sinful, rebellious nature of men and women. It proves us guilty. But if we are talking about an ability to lead men and women to God in the matter of salvation, general revelation does not do this, and therefore a fuller, special revelation is necessary.

Special Revelation

In several of his writings J. I. Packer talks about special revelation in three phases. First, there is *revelation in history*. Packer shows that God is a God who acts. This truth, perhaps more than anything else, clearly distinguishes the nature of Christianity from that of the other religions of the world. Christianity is not, as the Eastern religions would say of themselves, essentially a discipline by which we direct our thoughts and so order our lives that we progress in the direction of truth and eventually merge with the Eternal. Christianity is not so much a way of life as it is the intervention of God in history. We read in Genesis that God "created the heavens and the earth" (Gen. 1:1). "God created man" (Gen. 1:27). God called Abraham to create a special nation through whom a deliverer would come. God acted in the person of his Son, Jesus Christ, to die and rise again for our salvation.

Second, there is *revelation in writing*. We can see at once how essential this is. Because when we speak or write, as I just have, about the revelation of God in history—about God's creating the heavens and the earth, creating man, calling Abraham, and eventually sending Jesus Christ to die for our sin—we want to ask, But how do we know that God has done these things? We know through the Bible God has given us. First, God acts. Then God reveals himself in inspired writing, that we might under-stand what he has done.

Third, there is *revelation to the individual mind and heart*. This is the work of God's Holy Spirit by which our minds and hearts are opened to understand and receive what has been written. As a result, we are changed so that the Bible's teaching becomes no longer merely an academic thing but the actual point at which we hear God speaking. But again, notice the centrality of the Bible. We talk about the revelation of God in history, in writing, and in the personal illumination of the mind by the Holy Spirit. But the Bible is at the center of the process. The only way we know about God's acts in history is through the Bible, and the only point at which we hear the voice of God speaking to us personally is again through the Bible.

You say, Well, can't God speak otherwise? How about that voice from heaven? After all, Peter did hear a voice from heaven. Yes, that is true. But ask this question: Suppose you and I were together in a room and suddenly heard a voice from heaven. That would be a very moving experience. If that happened, I suppose there would be a moment of stunned silence. Then one of us would say, Did you hear that?

Yes, I heard it.

What did it say? At this point we might write the words down so we would remember them.

But now we ask the big question: Was that voice God's? I might think it was. You might think it was someone playing a practical joke. How are we to solve that dilemma? We cannot. So, although God can speak from heaven, and has on occasion, the only way we can verify that it is from God is to check it against the Bible, with what Peter called "the word . . . made more certain" (2 Peter 1:19).

In Jeremiah's day people were always coming up with fresh "revelations." These were, however, far from true revelations from God. They would say, Last night I had a dream, and in my dream God told me so and so. Jeremiah made fun of them, saying, I've heard what those prophets say, those who shout out, "I had a dream, I had a dream" (Jer. 23:25). They're lying prophets. Let them tell their dream. They're going to do it anyway. You can't stop them. Let them speak it. But Jeremiah made this contrast, "Let the prophet who has a dream tell his dream, but let the one who has my word speak it faithfully. For what has straw to do with grain? . . . Is not my word like fire . . . and like a hammer that breaks a rock in pieces?" (Jer. 23:28–29).

Inspiration

Another key term for understanding the nature of God's communication with us is *inspiration*. The most important verses to explain this are 2 Timothy 3:16–17: "All Scripture is God-breathed and is useful for teaching, rebuking, correcting and training in righteousness, so that the man of God may be thoroughly equipped for every good work." The key term is "God-breathed," the Greek word *theopneustos*.

Although *theopneustos* is traditionally translated "inspired," it is not as accurate as "God-breathed" for the simple reason that inspired suggests wrong ideas to most of us. We use inspiration in a very human way. We think of a poet writing a great poem and we say, He must certainly have been inspired to write that. We mean that his perception of reality, his understanding of human nature, and his gift for expression were above average in the writing of his poem. This is not what the Bible is talking about in this verse. Inspiration is man-centered. In

2 Timothy 3:16, Paul was not claiming that when Isaiah sat down to write his book, David to write his psalms, Moses to write the Pentateuch, or the Gospel writers to write their Gospels, these men had a higher degree of inspiration than most of us. Inspiration means far more than that one perceives things in a clearer way and expresses them more fluently and accurately than anybody has ever done before. Rather this verse is saying that the Bible is inspired in the sense that it is breathed out by God, so that what we have in the pages of the Bible is God's Word—fully and without exception.

B. B. Warfield wrote on this point:

> The Greek term has . . . nothing to say of inspiring or of inspiration; it speaks only of a "spiring" or "spiration." What it says of Scripture is, not that it is "breathed into by God" or is the product of the divine "inbreathing" into its human authors, but that it is breathed out by God. . . . When Paul declares, then, that "every scripture," or "all scripture" is the product of the divine breath, "is God-breathed," he asserts with as much energy as he could employ that Scripture is the product of a specifically divine operation.[2]

The idea of a breathed-out Bible becomes quite graphic when we realize that in many ancient languages the word for "breath" and the word for "spirit" are the same. In Hebrew the word is *ruach*. It refers to the Spirit of God, but it is also the word for breath. That is why, when we read in Genesis 1:2 that "the Spirit of God was hovering over the waters," the suggestion is sometimes made that this was a mighty breath or wind of God.[3]

In Latin the word is *spiritus*, which also means breath and spirit.

In Greek the word is *pneuma*.

We do not have many Hebrew words that carry over into English, because Hebrew is not part of our Western culture in the same way Greek and Latin are. So far as I know, we do not have any English words based upon the word *ruach*. But we do have words based upon *pneuma* and *spiritus*. We have pneumatic. A pneumatic drill is one that operates by air pressure. We have pneumonia, a disease of the "breath-box." So far as the Latin word is concerned, we have inspire, conspire, perspire and expire. When you are inspired, somebody breathes some of his breath into you. When people conspire, they put their heads together and breathe in and out together. When you perspire, you breathe out through your skin. When you expire, you breathe out for the last time: you die.

The words *pneuma, ruach,* and *spiritus* cannot be pronounced properly without breathing. So the sounds as well as the meaning of the words carry this thought. Inspiration is God breathing out. Is God using human agents? Yes, because Luke wrote with his vocabulary, John with his vocabulary, Isaiah with his vocabulary, and others. Men indeed wrote, but through them God breathed out, so that what we have in the Bible is not man's word but God's.

How did God do it? I think he did it in different ways. Moses received the Law on Mount Sinai where, at least at the first giving of the Law, God wrote on tablets of stone with his own finger, as the text describes (Ex. 31:18; Deut. 9:10). If this is meant to be literal and not merely figurative language, the effect was better than dictation. Moses just stood by and watched what God did.

One of the prophets said he heard the voice of God in his ears (Isa. 5:9). Others, I think, were essentially historians. That is, they gathered data and then composed their work much as any modern writer might. Luke wrote like this when he said at the beginning of his Gospel: "I myself have carefully investigated everything from the beginning" (Luke 1:3). He was saying, I looked up the documents. I talked to Mary to get the first two chapters of my Gospel. I talked to Paul about what he did when he was in Iconium and Lystra. I made notes. Clearly, the methodology of inspiration is different. But the important thing is that what was written was from God.

This view of inspiration is under attack today. Many people talk about inspiration, but they do not mean what the Bible means. They do not mean inspiration without error. They talk of partial inspiration or of the inspiration of ideas rather than words.

It is interesting to trace the spirit of unbelief as it has progressed in the church. Initially, Christian people assumed that if the Bible is the Word of God, it is perfect and without error, for God is perfect and does not lie. They said that the Bible is breathed out by God. However, eventually somebody came along who did not want to believe that. He countered, Well, it might be true that the Bible is inspired, and of course I believe that, because I'm a Christian. I do believe that the Bible is inspired. But it is not all equally inspired or inspired in every part. Soon many people were agreeing with this. The church then got together and said, Look! This is not what we understand the Bible to mean. Inspiration does not mean only some of the Scriptures are inspired. It means all the Scriptures. So the church introduced another word: "plenary," which means fullness or wholeness. At this point they talked about "plenary inspiration," or the Bible being the plenary inspired Word of God.

Next somebody said, That's true, if that's what the church says, and of course I'm a good churchman. I don't want to lose my pulpit if people find out I don't exactly believe it in the traditional way. I believe in plenary inspiration, but what I mean by that is the inspiration of ideas but not necessarily of the words. Hearing this, the church got together again and said, Do you mean that words don't count, that there might be error in the words, that perhaps the words aren't inspired? If you do, that's wrong. That's not what we mean by inspiration. So they added the word "verbal," meaning words, and talked about "verbal, plenary inspiration."

Farther along the time line of church history, another group of unbelievers reasoned, Well, yes, we believe that the words are inspired, too. That's all right. But, you know, even though they're inspired, there are nevertheless places where the words are wrong. They are not wrong in terms of their intention, but they mislead us if they are taken literally. Again the church objected. We are not going to allow that, it said. We'll have to use another word at this point. So they began to refer to it as "infallible verbal plenary inspiration."

Now we come to what people have been saying recently: Yes, yes, that's all true. The Bible is infallible. But there are still errors. At this point we have had to add the word "inerrant" in order to mean not merely the inspiration of the whole, or the inspiration of ideas, or the inspiration of words. We mean that the Bible is entirely trustworthy. It is the "inerrant, infallible, verbal, plenary inspired Word of God." When we do this, however, we are not teaching a new doctrine. We are spelling out, in language that speaks to the challenges of the hour, the truth Christians have believed down through the ages, namely, that the Bible is God's Word and is therefore perfect and truthful, as God himself is.

One other problem needs to be addressed. Some people say that because the Bible is given in human words it must have errors in it because, so the argument goes, to err is human. How do we handle this one?

We do not handle it by denying that the Bible is a human book as well as a divine one. Paul's vocabulary is different from Luke's. Luke's style is different from John's. The Gospels of Luke and John are certainly human books. Furthermore, it is important for us to recognize that they are, because the way to the mind of God is through the mind of the human author. If we do not understand what Luke is saying as a man, we do not understand what God is saying. We have to make distinctions between the way Luke talks and the way John talks. But this is not the same thing as admitting that the Bible has errors. It is not true that in any specific case it is necessary for a human being to err simply because he is human.

Take somebody who works in a printing company for example. This person's job is to produce a manual telling how to operate a washing machine. He works on it for a long time, describing how large the loads should be, what temperature the water should be, how to hook up the washer, and what buttons to push. He puts this information into a manual. While this person may be prone to error in many things, it is not intrinsically necessary that the manual have errors in it. It is quite possible, in this specific instance, that the manual produced will be a totally inerrant document.

True, we do err most of the time. It is hard to produce even a little manual that is utterly without error. I admit that when we turn to the Word of God, the production of an inerrant Bible is a tall order. It was written by numerous authors over a period of fifteen hundred years on all sorts of subjects. The point is that it is not metaphysically impossible that this could be done. It is possible, as the International Council on Biblical Inerrancy has stated, that "what Scripture says, God says—through human agents and without error."[4]

You Must Be Born Again

After *revelation* and *inspiration*, the most important word for understanding how God speaks to us is *regeneration*. In our natural or unregenerate state we cannot understand spiritual things even if God reveals them clearly. More than that, we are even hostile to them.

Consider the occasion in John 3:1–15 when Nicodemus, a ruler of the Jews, came to Jesus and began to engage him in theological discussion. Nicodemus was a man who was learned in the Old Testament and no doubt highly regarded by his contemporaries as a knowledgeable and pious person. As he heard Jesus speaking, Nicodemus recognized that he was extraordinary. Moreover, he saw Jesus performing miracles, and miracles are done by God. To the ruler, God was authenticating Jesus as a teacher, and he was obviously a person to whom he should listen and from whom he should learn.

Nicodemus went to Jesus by night and said, in effect, I want you to know, Jesus, that I am not entirely ignorant of spiritual things. I am aware that you are a teacher come from God. And the reason I know this is that you are doing miracles, and no one can do such miracles unless God is with him. God is with you, and you are a person from whom I should learn.

What did Jesus say after Nicodemus had approached him on that basis? Did Jesus say, Congratulations, Nicodemus, you have certainly been able to think clearly at a time when many of the lesser people of your generation seem incapable of it; you have seen that I am indeed a teacher come from God; let's go on from this point and together seek out the truth from God.

No, he did not! Jesus' answer must have been devastating: Nicodemus, you are utterly ignorant of spiritual things. You are ignorant because you have not been born again. Until you are, there is no point in our even discussing the matters you have in mind.

Later in 1 Corinthians 2:14, Paul explained why this is the case: "The man without the Spirit does not accept the things that come from the Spirit of God, for they are foolishness to him, and he cannot understand them, because they are spiritually discerned." Since it requires the Spirit to understand spiritual things, no one who is not born again can understand what God has to say.

It is by means of the Bible that God regenerates a person. Once again we see the Spirit and the Word working together. Peter wrote, "You have been born again, not of perishable seed, but of imperishable, through the living and enduring word of God" (1 Peter 1:23). By the power of the Holy Spirit, God takes Bible truths and applies them to our hearts to make us spiritually alive. Then, being made spiritually alive, we understand, respond to, and obey the teachings of the Bible.

When Peter mentioned "seed," he was not talking about the kind of seeds we plant in the ground. He was referring to human semen and suggesting that God engenders spiritual children much like a human father engenders a human child. When a child is conceived, the semen of the father unites with the egg or ovum of the mother. Life begins to grow. In spiritual conception, the sperm is God's Word. The egg is faith. But even that is not of us in the ultimate analysis. Faith comes from God. Paul wrote that faith was "not from [ourselves], it is the gift of God" (Eph. 2:8).

God first places the ovum of saving faith into the heart of a man or woman. Then he uses his Word to penetrate the egg of faith, and a new spiritual life begins. It is a small thing at first. Often we are not even sure it is there. But it is there, and the person soon begins to feel the tuggings of the new life within. Before, he was not interested in spiritual things. Now he is. Before, he was not attracted to Christians or the Bible. Now he wants to spend time with both. Things that never made sense before now begin to make sense. Finally, the time comes when a preacher declares, If you want to receive Jesus as your Savior, if you want to commit your life to him, raise your hand [or stand up]. The person does. Someone says, You've just been born again. Actually, he or she was already spiritually alive, like a baby in the womb. The response was merely the birth cry. It is not the cry that makes the baby come alive but the Word of God producing new life in the heart.

Illumination

Earlier, I suggested several problems in understanding general revelation from the point of view of effective communication. First, it is a limited revelation, revealing only certain things about God and not the whole of the gospel. Second, we do not respond to general revelation because we cannot understand it, and we do not like the God who is revealed there. Then we looked at special revelation, that is the revelation of God in Scripture, and discovered that special revelation overcomes the first of these two problems.

The general revelation of God in nature tells us only about God's existence and power. In the Bible God specifically records his actions and interprets these actions for us. He lays out the whole gospel, and everything we need to know is before us. Yet, this knowledge is ineffective for salvation because we still cannot understand or receive what God is saying. To deal with this second problem, God gives us a new nature through the miracle of the new birth. At this point we might think that God has done everything necessary, but there is one thing more. Now that we are able to understand his Word, God offers us further illumination through the work of his Holy Spirit.

This is the ground Paul covered in 1 Corinthians 2:6–16 when he spoke about special revelation as "God's secret wisdom" (v. 7), a personal communication to us by God's Spirit (v. 10). Even at this point, however, we continue to need help as we study God's Word. We need God-given understanding. So Paul continued, "We have not received the spirit of the world but the Spirit who is from God, that we may understand what God has freely given us" (v. 12). It is through the Spirit that "we have the mind of Christ" (v. 16).

A great story preserved in Luke 24 illustrates these truths. Jesus had risen from the dead and had begun to appear to his followers. Two of these, Cleopas and possibly his wife Mary, were returning to their home town of Emmaus when Jesus drew near them on the road. They did not recognize him. When asked why they were downcast, they replied by telling him what had happened in Jerusalem at the time of the Passover.

They told him about Jesus: "He was a prophet, powerful in word and deed before God and all the people" (v. 19). They told him how the chief priests and rulers "handed him over to be sentenced to death, and . . . crucified him" (v. 20). They related that they had been in Jerusalem that very morning and had heard reports from the women who had been to the tomb, that Jesus' body was gone and that angels had appeared proclaiming that he was alive! But this had failed to interest them. They did not believe in resurrections. They had not even bothered to go to the tomb to see for themselves, although it was only a short distance away. So far as they were concerned the dream was over. Jesus was dead and they were going home.

But Jesus began to talk to them and explain his mission, teaching them from the Scriptures. He said, "How foolish you are, and how slow to believe all that the prophets have spoken! Did not the Christ have to suffer these things and then enter his glory?" (vv. 25–6). Then, beginning with Moses and going through all the prophets "he explained to them what was said in the Scriptures concerning himself" (vv. 13–27).

This story (and its sequel) contains three great revelations, called "openings." The first, mentioned specifically later, is the opening of Scripture. After Jesus had disappeared from their sight, these two disciples said to each other, "Were not our hearts burning within us while he talked with us on the road and opened the Scriptures to us?" (v. 32). That is the point at which Jesus began. Jesus did not say, Look, here I am. I'm Jesus. Can't you tell? No, he took them to the Word of God. He opened the Scriptures. He said, Look at what the Bible says. Look at this passage. Look at that passage.

Second, "their eyes were opened and they recognized him" (v. 31). This was the second step. First, he opened the Scriptures. Then, as the Scriptures were opened and as the Holy Spirit (in this case Jesus himself) continued his work, their eyes were opened and they perceived Jesus to be the Savior.

The third of these three openings is mentioned in verse 45. The Emmaus disciples had gone back to Jerusalem where Jesus appeared to them again. The verse says, "Then he opened their minds so they could understand the Scriptures." Do you see how it works? There is a progression of Word, eyes, and mind. In every case communication goes back to the Word of God and God's Spirit.

One of the basic problems of our time is subjectivity. I am sure that every Christian at one time or another, perhaps many times, has said or thought, God is leading me to do so and so. We may even put it in stronger terms, God told me to do so and so. If we mean that the Holy Spirit has spoken from heaven and given us fresh revelation unrelated to the Bible, a revelation that we should do so and so, we are making a serious error. The Holy

Spirit does not do that today. And, if he did, there would be no way of testing it. You could receive one revelation and I could receive another. There would be no way of knowing who had the true communication. Apart from the Bible we have no way of verifying that kind of revelation. On the other hand, if we mean that God has directed us in accordance with the principles of his written revelation, then we may be on the right track, because God most certainly does lead that way. God leads his people through the Word.

And that is the way it ought to be. No matter how intense our experiences, no matter how acute our perceptions of what we think God would have us do, we cannot be certain God has spoken unless our revelation is based on Scripture. The Holy Spirit teaches through Scripture. It is only through this assurance that we can properly sense the will of God and become strong as Christian people.

3

POSITIVE EVIDENCE FOR THE BIBLE

Perhaps the title of this chapter should read: Positive Evidence for the Bible Being the Word of God. We need to talk about the Bible being the Word of God, for there is a sense in which, if we establish that point, we have established everything else about what the Bible is.

A decade or so ago the battle for the Bible focused on the issue of inerrancy. Only recently have people been irrational enough to imagine that the Bible can be from God and at the same time errant. Before this, if people believed that the Bible was not the Word of God, neither errancy nor inerrancy mattered. And if it was the Word of God, inerrancy followed naturally.

God is a God of truth. God does not speak falsehood. So if the Bible is the Word of God—not merely something that testifies to the Word of God or contains the Word of God, but really is the Word of God—then it is truthful and authoritative in all its parts. Unfortunately, since today is an irrational age, points like this have to be made individually.

God's Word or Man's Word

There are really only three basic positions in regard to the Bible: (1) the Bible is the Word of God, (2) it is the words of mere men only, (3) it is a combination of both.

The first is *the classic, evangelical doctrine,* the view believed throughout church history. Even when there were debates about the nature of Jesus Christ, man, or justification, the people involved always appealed to the Bible. Even the heretics regarded the Bible as the Word of God. They disagreed with church teachings, and the heretics had to be corrected as the church studied the issue, allowing the Holy Spirit to speak through the Word to the people of that day. But everyone stood by the conviction that the Bible is God's Word and is therefore inerrant in whatever it does teach. Only in recent times has this position been abandoned.

The classic, evangelical view that the Bible is the Word of God does not deny that it is also expressed in human language. Some people who have fallen into thinking that the Bible was somehow dictated by God have difficulty explaining how the style of one book differs from the style of another book. This problem is solved by acknowledging that the Word of God comes to us through human authors, who wrote according to their own style and vocabulary. When talking in these terms, we must acknowledge the sense in which the Bible is also the words of men. But, of course, it is more than that.

When we talk about the classic church view—that the Bible is the Word of God—we mean that by the process of inspiration, which we freely admit we do not fully understand, God so guided the human authors that the result, in the whole and in the parts, is what God desired to be expressed. So the Bible is the Word of God from beginning to end, and it is entirely truthful because God is truthful.

The second view, that the Bible is the word of man, is *the view of liberalism and neoorthodoxy*. Although many of the neoorthodox theologians gave great attention to the Bible and were willing to listen to it, neoorthodoxy said that God is so transcendent, so far above us, so separated from where we are, that he does not actually speak in human words but rather reveals himself in ways we cannot even discuss. So what we have in the Bible is men testifying in their own words to what they believed God said in this non-verbal fashion.

The third position is the one we are wrestling with today. This is *the view that the Bible is the Word of God and the word of men combined*. This view says that when you read the Bible, you find things that have certainly come from God and are therefore truthful. But you must admit that you also find things that are not truthful, things you know to be in error. Because God does not speak that which is untruthful, these things must have come from human beings and from human beings alone. In other words, in the Bible we have a combination of divine words and human words, and it is the task of scholarship to sort these out.

What happens in that framework is that the scholar becomes God. That is, he becomes the authority who tells Christians what is true and what is not true, what is of God and what is not of God, what people are to believe and what they are not to believe. The danger here is that because we are sinners, we always weed out those things we do not want to hear. Those sayings of God that are there to correct the church, discipline our thinking, and influence our lives are often the parts we decide to erase. That is what happens when one departs from the evangelical view.

Five Lines of Evidence

The Teaching of Christ

Five lines of evidence support the assertion that the Bible truly is the Word of God—truthful and inerrant. The most important one is that this is the teaching of Jesus Christ. Jesus Christ as the Son of God speaks to us, not as an errant authority but as an inerrant, infallible authority. If Jesus is who he claimed to be, and if Jesus truly taught those teachings attributed to him in the Word of God, then we can believe the Bible to be the Word of God because Jesus believed it to be the Word of God.

This argument is sufficient by itself. If you think about it, you can easily understand why. Suppose the Lord Jesus Christ was with us in person, and suppose we could hear him address us, saying that the Bible is the Word of God and is therefore absolutely truthful. At that point there would probably be many questions we would want to ask him. We might say, Well, yes, Jesus, but as I read the Bible there are some things I don't understand. For example, in the accounts of the Resurrection I read things that seem to me to be contradictions. One of the Gospel writers will tell about one woman being present at the tomb while another will tell about several women being present. I don't understand. Would you please explain this problem?

This is the kind of question we might legitimately ask the Lord, and we would probably expect a very simple answer. He could presumably explain the situation exactly. I might add that this is also the kind of question we ask again and again when studying the Word of God. It is the way to grow. We look at the difficulties, and we wrestle with them. As one who teaches the Bible Sunday by Sunday, paragraph by paragraph, sometimes verse by verse or even line by line, I have learned my greatest lessons when wrestling with things that seem very difficult at the start. So, this kind of question is entirely proper.

But if the Lord Jesus Christ were standing with us in person and said, "The Bible is the Word of God and is therefore truthful and inerrant in all it says," then we could not ask him whether the Bible is the Word of God and truthful and inerrant in all it says.

The word of Jesus as Jehovah in human flesh is sufficient in and of itself. Whatever problems we face, whatever difficulties we may perceive, whatever lack of understanding we have, on this point at least we would find ourselves utterly united and convinced. If Jesus Christ is who he claims to be, if he is who the church has always confessed him to be, namely, the Lord of Glory, we must accept what he says.

So the question becomes, Does the Lord Jesus Christ actually testify to the Scriptures along these lines? I am sure you know the answer to this question because it has been given many times. B. B. Warfield has written magnificent essays on this subject.[1] There are whole books on it.[2] When we honestly turn to the Scriptures to view the recorded testimony of Jesus Christ, we find Jesus taught the highest of all possible views of Scripture. He regarded it as having come from God, as speaking with divine authority, and as binding even upon Jesus' own actions. Jesus read Scripture in order to conform to it and thereby conform to the will of the Father in heaven.

When our Lord was tempted by the devil in the wilderness, he replied by quoting Scripture. He did not get into a theological argument. He did not descend to philosophy. He did not say to the devil, I want to know your credentials when you present these temptations. He simply quoted from the Book of Deuteronomy again and again, saying, This is what God says.

As a matter of fact, Jesus was so successful that the devil himself got into the act. When Satan tempted the Lord to turn stones into bread, Jesus replied, "Man does not live on bread alone, but on every word that comes from the mouth of God" (Matt. 4:4), quoting from Deuteronomy 8:3. The devil then said, in effect, Ah, I see you are a student of Scripture! I am a student of Scripture myself, and in that respect I'd like to call your attention to something that occurs in the Psalms. Those verses say, "He will command his angels concerning you, and they will lift you up in their hands, so that you will not strike your foot against a stone" (Ps. 91:11–12). It does say that, doesn't it, Jesus? I'm not quoting incorrectly now, am I?

No, you're quoting it correctly.

Well, then, let's do it! Let's not only be orthodox in our profession; let's put our actions where our mouth is. Let's go up on the temple, and you jump off. If that verse is true, then God will pick you up so you don't strike your foot against a stone.

This temptation did not throw the Lord off one bit because he knew what the devil was trying to do by quoting God against God. The Lord was too good a Bible scholar for that.

Jesus replied, No, you can't do that because there's a verse in the Bible covering that situation, too. The verse I want to bring to your attention, Satan, is Deuteronomy 6:16, which says, "Do not put the Lord your God to the test." Later Jesus also quoted from Deuteronomy 6:13.

In Matthew 22:23–32 Jesus silenced the Sadducees' question about the heavenly status of marriage and the reality of the resurrection in the same way. He rebuked them by saying that they did not know the Scriptures or the power of God. Then he quoted from Exodus 3:6: "I am the God of your father, the God of Abraham, the God of Isaac and the God of Jacob." The Lord explained that this verse taught that God is "not the God of the dead, but of the living, for to him all are alive" (Luke 20:38).

Jesus appealed to Scripture to support his actions, to defend his cleansing of the temple (Mark 11:15–17), and to explain his submitting to the cross (Matt. 26:53–54). He taught that "the Scripture cannot be broken" (John 10:35). He declared, "Until heaven and earth disappear, not the smallest letter, not the last stroke of a pen, will by any means disappear from the Law until everything is accomplished" (Matt. 5:18).

The last verse literally reads "not an iota, not a tittle." The *iota* or *yodh* was the smallest letter of the Hebrew alphabet, the letter we would transliterate by an "i" or a "y." In written Hebrew it resembled a comma, though it was written near the top of the letters rather than near the bottom. The *tittle* was what we would call a serif, the tiny projection on letters that distinguishes a roman type face from a more modern one. In many Bibles Psalm 119 is divided into twenty-two sections, each beginning with a different letter of the Hebrew alphabet. The English reader can see what a tittle is by comparing the Hebrew letter before verse 9 with the Hebrew letter before verse 81. The first letter is a *beth*. The second is a *kaph*. The only difference between them is the serif. The same feature distinguishes *daleth* from *resh* and *vau* from *zayin*. So according to Jesus, not even an "i" or a "serif" of the Law would be lost until the whole Law was fulfilled.

What can possibly give the Law this character? Obviously nothing human for all things human pass away. The only thing that can possibly give the Law this imperishable quality is that it is divine. The reason it will not pass away is that it is the word of the true, living, and eternal God. This is the substance of Christ's teaching.

Jesus also saw his life as the fulfillment of Scripture and thus consciously submitted himself to it. He began his ministry with a quotation from Isaiah 61:1–2: "The Spirit of the Lord is on me, because he has anointed me to preach good news to the poor. He has sent me to proclaim freedom for the prisoners and recovery of sight for the blind, to release the oppressed, to proclaim the year of the Lord's favor" (Luke 4:18–19). When he had finished reading he put the scroll down and said, "Today this scripture is fulfilled in your hearing" (v. 21). Jesus was claiming to be the Messiah, the one about whom Isaiah had written, and was identifying his ministry with the lines set out for it in Scripture.

In John 5 Jesus was talking to the Jewish rulers about authority. His climax had to do with Scripture. The Lord said that nobody would ever believe him who had not first believed the writings of Moses: "You diligently study the Scriptures because you think that by them you possess eternal life. These are the Scriptures that testify about me. . . . Do not think I will accuse you before the Father. Your accuser is Moses, on whom your hopes are set. If you believed Moses, you would believe me, for he wrote about me. But since you do not believe what he wrote, how are you going to believe what I say?" (John 5:39, 45–47).

At the end of his life, as he was hanging on the cross, Jesus was again thinking of Scripture. He said, "My God, my God, why have you forsaken me?" (Matt. 27:46, a quotation from Ps. 22:1). He said that he was thirsty. They gave him a sponge filled with vinegar to fulfill Psalm 69:21. Three days later, after the Resurrection, he was on the way to Emmaus with two of his disciples, chiding them because they had not used Scripture to understand the necessity of his suffering. He said, "How foolish you are, and how slow of heart to believe all that the prophets have spoken! Did not the Christ have to suffer these things and then enter his glory?" Then "beginning with Moses and all the Prophets, he explained to them what was said in all the Scriptures concerning himself" (Luke 24:25–27).

On the basis of these and other passages, it is clear that Jesus highly esteemed the Old Testament and constantly submitted to it as to an authoritative revelation. He taught that Scripture bore witness to him just as he bore witness to it. Because it is the Word of God, Jesus assumed its complete truthfulness, in the whole and to the smallest part.

Jesus endorsed the New Testament as well, although in a way different from his endorsement of the Old Testament. He foresaw the writing of the New Testament and made special provision for it by choosing and authorizing the apostles to receive and record the new revelation. He said to them, "But the Counselor, the Holy Spirit, whom the Father will send in my name, will teach you all things and will remind you of everything I have said to you" (John 14:26). He said, "I have much more to say to you, more than you can now bear. But when he, the Spirit of truth, comes, he will guide you into all truth. He will not speak on his own; he will speak only what he hears, and he will tell you what is yet to come. He will bring glory to me by taking from what is mine and making it known to you" (John 16:12–14).

The apostles fulfilled their commission by giving us the New Testament. What's more, the early church recognized the role of the apostles for when it came time to declare officially those books to be included in the canon of the New Testament, the decisive factor was whether or not they were written by the apostles or bore apostolic endorsement.

One possible objection arises at this point. Someone might dismiss this argument as circular reasoning. Circular reasoning is reasoning in which one argument is supported by another, which is supported by the first. It does not go anywhere; it is faulty. Suppose I say, "You know, I'm very hungry; I'd like to go out and get something to eat. Do you know a good place to go?" And Joe says, "Oh, yes, you ought to go to the Third Avenue Deli." Then, suppose I ask, "How do you know that's a good place to eat? Have you eaten there?"

Joe replies, "No, I've never been there, but Sam raves about it."

I approach Sam and say, "Sam, I hear the Third Avenue Deli's a good place to eat. Is it?"

"Yes."

"How do you know? Have you eaten there?"

"No, I've never eaten there, but Joe told me it's a great place and I trust Joe."

What was learned in such an exchange? Nothing! Because it is a circular argument. Joe supports Sam; Sam supports Joe; the argument does not go anywhere.

Some people maintain this is what we are doing when we refer to Jesus' belief in Scripture. They say, Look, you are quoting the teachings of Jesus to establish the authority of the Bible. But the reason you believe the teachings of Jesus is that you believe the Bible. In other words, you go to the Bible to get your view of Jesus, and from Jesus you get your view of the Bible. However logical this may sound, that is not what we are doing, as I want to show.

Follow this step by step.

First, when we talk about the teaching of Jesus Christ we do not start with the assumption that the Bible is inerrant or even that it is the Word of God. We begin with the Bible as an historical document. We know it is ancient. It dates back almost two thousand years in its New Testament form and more than that in its Old Testament form. When we study it, we find it

believable. Under the most careful scrutiny and analysis we find
it to be extraordinarily reliable. Above all, it offers a consistent,
believable picture of Jesus Christ. We do not start with the Bible
as the Word of God or with inerrancy. We begin simply by saying it is a reliable, historical book.

Second, the Bible points directly to Jesus. According to his witnesses, he was like nobody else who has ever lived. As a matter of
fact, the only explanation we have for a man who could do the
things the Bible says he did is that he was more than a man. In
fact, he was precisely who he claimed to be: God incarnate.

Third, if this man about whom the Bible speaks is God incarnate, then what he teaches on any subject must be true, because
God speaks truth.

So we ask, fourth, What does he teach about the Bible? In
answer, he teaches that the Bible is the Word of God.

The fifth point in the argument is this: We believe that the
Bible is the Word of God because Jesus teaches it and because
Jesus, as the incarnate Son of God, is an unimpeachable author-
ity. Such an argument is not circular.

Of course, there is a great deal more involved. When we study
the Bible it is never simply a case of studying an historical document because the Bible is God's Word and the Holy Spirit
speaks through it. The Holy Spirit teaches us things we would
not have otherwise believed. We readily admit that. The point
I am making is that it is not a circular argument to reason that
the greatest evidence that the Bible is the Word of God is Christ's
testimony.

The Bible Itself

The second line of evidence that the Bible is the Word of
God is the nature of the Bible itself. The Bible is not like other
books. One thing that strikes us is *the Bible's teaching about itself.*
Many people, even those who have a defective view of Scripture, come to the Bible for its teachings on Jesus, God, justification, sanctification, salvation, eschatology, and other things.

But when it comes to the Bible's teaching about the Bible, they draw the line. They say, We don't credit the Bible at that point. Such a procedure is inconsistent. If the Bible can be trusted to speak about Jesus, God, salvation, and eschatology, it can certainly be trusted to speak about itself. And when you approach the Bible to see what it says about itself, you soon find thousands of places in which it claims to be the Word of God.

In the Old Testament the phrase "Thus saith the Lord" occurs more than two thousand times. The apostle Paul says the same thing in the New Testament, "We speak, not in words taught us by human wisdom but in words taught by the Spirit, expressing spiritual truths in spiritual words" (1 Cor. 2:13). That is a great claim of inspiration! The Bible contains the most sublime teachings and morals of any book ever written. What can account for a book like this, a book with exalted moral content, which does not hesitate to expose the sin of man and yet claims to be from God? Who can explain this kind of a book? Who could have written it if God did not?

Thomas Watson, one of the great English Puritans, wrote: "I wonder whence the Scriptures should come, if not from God. Bad men could not be the authors of it. Would their minds be employed in indicting such holy lines? Would they declare so fiercely against sin? Could good men be the authors of it? Could they write in such a strain? Or could it stand with their grace to counterfeit God's name and put 'Thus saith the Lord' to a book of their own devising?"[3] If good men did not write the Bible and if bad men did not write it, the only conclusion is that men did not write it. Who did? God alone, as the Scriptures claim.

The nature of the Bible also concerns *the Bible's unity*. This is an old argument, but it deserves strong notice. Here is one book comprised of sixty-six different books, written over a period of about fifteen hundred years by about forty different authors. These authors were not alike; they came from different levels of society and from diverse backgrounds. Some were kings. Others were statesmen, priests, prophets, a tax collector, a physician, a tentmaker, fishermen. When asked about any particular subject, these writers would have had views as diverse as the opinions of men living today. Yet together they produced a work of marvelous unity in its doctrines, historical viewpoints, ethics, and expectations. It is, in short, a single story of divine redemption begun in Israel, centered in Jesus Christ, and culminating at the end of history.

Moreover, the nature of this unity is important. As R. A. Torrey noted,

> It is not a superficial unity, but a profound unity. On the surface, we often find apparent discrepancy and disagreement, but as we study, the apparent discrepancy and disagreement disappear, and the deep underlying unity appears. The more deeply we study, the more complete do we find the unity to be. The unity is also an organic one—that is, it is not the unity of a dead thing, like a stone, but of a living thing, like a plant. In the early books of the Bible we have the germinant thought; as we go on we have the plant, and further on the bud, and then the blossom, and then the ripened fruit. In Revelation we find the ripened fruit of Genesis.[4]

Only one thing accounts for this unity. Behind the efforts of the more than forty human authors is the one perfect, sovereign, and guiding mind of God.

The nature of the Bible also involves its *uncommon accuracy*. To be sure, this does not prove the Bible is divine—mere men can also be quite accurate—but it is what we should expect if the Bible is the result of God's own effort.

We may take the Gospel of Luke and the Book of Acts as two examples. These books were an attempt to set forth an "orderly account" of Jesus' life and of the rapid expansion of the early Christian church (Luke 1:1–4; Acts 1:1–2). This was an enormous undertaking. It would be in our day. It was especially so in ancient times, when there were no newspapers or reference books. In fact, there were few written documents of any kind. Yet, in spite of this lack of written data, Luke accurately charted

the growth of the church from an insignificant religious movement in a far corner of the Roman Empire to the Christian congregations rapidly growing in most of the major cities of the
Empire within forty years of the death and resurrection of Jesus
Christ. Does Luke's work succeed? It does so remarkably.

For one thing, his books accurately handle official titles and
the corresponding spheres of influence. This has been docu-
mented by F. F. Bruce of the University of Manchester, England,
in a small work entitled *The New Testament Documents: Are They
Reliable?* Bruce writes,

> One of the most remarkable tokens of his accuracy is his sure
> familiarity with the proper titles of all the notable persons who
> are mentioned in his pages. This was by no means such an easy
> feat in his day as it is in ours, when it is so simple to consult con-
> venient books of reference. The accuracy of Luke's use of the
> various titles in the Roman empire has been compared to the
> easy and confident way in which an Oxford man in ordinary con-
> versation will refer to the Heads of colleges by their proper
> titles—the *Provost* of Oriel, the *Master* of Balliol, the *Rector* of
> Exeter, the *President* of Magdalen, and so on.
>
> A non-Oxonian like the present writer never feels quite at
> home with the multiplicity of these Oxford titles.[5]

Luke feels at home with the Roman titles and never gets them
wrong.

Bruce adds that Luke had another difficulty because the titles
often did not remain the same for any great length of time. For
example, a province might move from administration by a direct
representative of the emperor to a senatorial government, and
would then be governed by a proconsul rather than an imperial
legate. Cyprus, an imperial province until 22 B.C., became a senatorial province in that year and was no longer governed by an
imperial legate but rather by a proconsul. Thus, when Paul and
Barnabas arrived in Cyprus about A.D. 47, it was the "proconsul" Sergius Paulus who greeted them (Acts 13:7).

Achaia was a senatorial province from 27 B.C. to A.D. 15, and again subsequent to A.D. 44. Hence, Luke refers to Gallio, the Roman ruler in Greece, as "the proconsul of Achaia" (Acts 18:12), the title of the Roman representative during the time of Paul's visit to Corinth but not during the twenty-nine years prior to A.D. 44.

This kind of testimony can be multiplied almost indefinitely. For example, in Acts 19:38 the town clerk of Ephesus tried to calm the rioting citizens by referring them to the Roman authorities. "There are proconsuls," he said, using the plural. This might be thought to be a mistake at first since there was only one Roman proconsul in a given area at a time. But an examination shows that shortly before the rioting at Ephesus, Junius Silanus, the proconsul, had been murdered by messengers from Agrippina, the mother of Nero, who was still an adolescent. Since the new proconsul had not yet arrived in Ephesus, the town clerk's vagueness may have been intentional or may even have referred to the two emissaries, Helius and Celer, who were the apparent successors to Silanus' power.

Similarly, Luke captured the tone of the city in a time of internal disturbance, just as elsewhere he also captured the tones of Antioch, Jerusalem, Rome, and other cities, each with its own unique flavor.

Archaeology has substantiated the Bible's extraordinary reliability for the writings of Luke as well as for other documents. A plaque has been found in Delphi identifying Gallio as the proconsul in Corinth at the precise time of Paul's visit to the city. The pool of Bethesda, containing five porticoes, has been found approximately seventy feet below the present level of the city of Jerusalem. It is mentioned in John 5:2, but it had been lost to view until recent times through the destruction of the city by the armies of Titus in A.D. 70. The Pavement of Judgment, *Gabbatha*, mentioned in John 19:13, has been uncovered.

There are also ancient documents from Dura, Ras Shamra, Egypt, and the Dead Sea. In recent years reports of remarkable finds at Tell Mardikh in northwest Syria, the site of ancient Ebla, have been received. Thus far, fifteen thousand tablets dating from approximately 2300 B.C. (200–500 years before Abraham) have been discovered. Hundreds of names such as Abram, Israel, Esau, David, Yahweh, and Jerusalem are found in them. These tablets will undoubtedly throw much light on customs in the days of the patriarchs.

As recently as 1993, newspapers carried reports of the discovery of a victory stele in northern Israel near the Syrian border bearing the Aramaic words for "house of David." Although David was the greatest king and one of the most highly regarded heroes of Israel, this was the first clear reference to him outside the pages of the Bible. So the data continues to come in.

Prophecy

The third evidence for the Bible as the Word of God is prophecy. Although this is a large subject, it is possible to illustrate the nature of the argument briefly.

Explicit verbal prophecies concern the future of the Jewish people (including things that have already occurred and some that have not yet occurred), the future of the Gentile nations, and above all the coming of the Lord Jesus Christ, first to die and then afterward to return in power and great glory. The five passages of Isaiah 53; Micah 5:2; Daniel 9:25–27; Jeremiah 23:5–6; and Psalm 16:8–11 predict the coming of Jesus. They tell us the exact time of his coming, the exact place of his birth, the family into which he should be born, the condition of his family at the time, the manner of his reception by Israel, the fact, the method, and details of his death and burial, his resurrection following his burial, and his ascension subsequent to his resurrection.

E. Schuyler English, chairman of the editorial committee of *The New Scofield Reference Bible* (1967) and editor-in-chief of *The Pilgrim Bible* (1948), claimed that more than twenty Old Testament predictions were fulfilled within a twenty-four-hour period at the time of Jesus' crucifixion.[6]

Some scholars are attacking many of these prophecies, and attempts have been made to redate some Old Testament books to bring them nearer to the time of Christ. But the most radical and destructive critic can take these prophecies to the very latest date imagined, and they are still hundreds of years before the birth of Christ. Moreover, their cumulative witness is devastating. The only way to account for these fulfilled prophecies is through the existence of a sovereign God, who revealed in advance what was to happen through Jesus and who saw to it that this actually took place.

The Bible's Preservation

The fourth reason for believing the Bible to be the Word of God is its extraordinary preservation down through the many centuries of Old Testament and church history. Today, after the Bible has been translated in part or whole into many hundreds of languages, some with multiple versions, and after millions of copies have been printed and distributed, it would be nearly impossible to destroy it.

But such conditions did not always prevail. Until the time of the Reformation, the Bible's text was preserved by the laborious and time-consuming process of copying it over and over again by hand, at first onto papyrus sheets and then onto parchments. Throughout much of this time, the Bible was an object of extreme hatred by many in authority. These men tried to stamp it out, but the text survived. In the early days of the church, Celsus, Prophyry, and Lucien tried to destroy it by arguments. Later the emperors Diocletian and Julian tried to destroy it by force. At several points it was actually a capital offense to possess a copy of the Bible. Yet the text has survived.

If the Bible had only been the thoughts or work of mere men, it would have been eliminated long ago, as other books have been. But it has endured, fulfilling the words of Jesus, who said, "Heaven and earth will pass away, but my words will never pass away" (Matt. 24:35).

Isaiah likewise wrote, "The grass withers and the flowers fall, but the word of our God stands forever" (Isa. 40:8).

Transformation of Men and Women

The final reason for believing the Bible is the Word of God is its ability to change even the worst men and women and transform them into a blessing to all who know them. The Bible speaks of this power when it says,

> The law of the Lord is perfect,
>   reviving the soul.
> The statutes of the Lord are trustworthy,
>   making wise the simple.
> The precepts of the Lord are right,
>   giving joy to the heart.
> The commandments of the Lord are radiant,
>   giving light to the eyes.
> The fear of the Lord is pure,
>   enduring forever.
> The ordinances of the Lord are sure
>   and altogether righteous.
>
> Psalm 19:7–9

Does the Bible actually transform men and women, turning them into godly persons? It obviously does. Prostitutes have been reformed. Drunkards have become sober. The proud have been humbled. Dishonest men have become models of integrity. Weak men have become strong—all because of the transformation wrought in them by God as these sinners heard and applied Scripture.

Early in his ministry Harry A. Ironside lived in the San Francisco Bay area and worked with some Christians called Brethren. One evening as he was walking through the city, he came upon a group of Salvation Army workers holding a meeting on the corner of Market and Grant Avenues. When they recognized

Ironside, they asked him to give his testimony. He did, telling how God had saved him through faith in the bodily death and literal resurrection of Jesus.

As he spoke, Ironside noticed at the edge of the crowd a well-dressed man who had taken a card from his pocket and was writing something on it. As Ironside finished his talk the man came forward, lifted his hat, and very politely handed Ironside the card. On one side was his name. Ironside immediately recognized it. The man was one of the early socialists who had made a name for himself lecturing for socialism and against Christianity. As Ironside turned the card over he read, "Sir, I challenge you to debate with me the question 'Agnosticism versus Christianity' in the Academy of Science Hall next Sunday afternoon at four o'clock. I will pay all expenses."

Ironside reread the card aloud and then replied, "I am very much interested in this challenge. Frankly, I am already scheduled for another meeting next Lord's Day afternoon at three o'clock, but I think it will be possible for me to get through with that in time to reach the Academy of Science Hall by four, or if necessary I would arrange to have another speaker substitute for me at the meeting already advertised. Therefore I will be glad to agree to this debate on the following conditions: namely, that in order to prove that this gentleman has something worth debating about, he will promise to bring with him to the hall next Sunday two people, whose qualifications I will give in a moment, as proof that agnosticism is of real value in changing human lives and building true character.

"First, he must promise to bring with him one man who has been what we commonly call a 'down-and-outer.' I am not particular as to the exact nature of the sins that once wrecked his life and made him an outcast from society—whether a drunkard, or a criminal of some kind, or a victim of his sensual appetite. But I want a man who for years was under the power of evil habits from which he could not deliver himself and who once entered one of this man's meetings to hear his glorification of agnosticism and his denunciations of the Bible and Christianity, and whose heart and mind were so deeply stirred that he went away from that meeting saying, 'Henceforth, I too am an agnostic!' and, as a result of imbibing that particular philosophy found a new power in his life. The sins he once loved he now hates, and righteousness and goodness are now the ideals of his life. He is now an entirely new man, a credit to himself, and an asset to society—all because he is an agnostic.

"Secondly, I would like my opponent to promise to bring with him one woman—I think he may have more difficulty in finding a woman than a man—who was once a poor, wrecked, characterless outcast, the slave of evil passions, and the victim of man's corrupt living, perhaps one who had lived for years in some evil resort, utterly lost, ruined, and wretched because of her life of sin. This woman must also have entered a hall where this man was loudly proclaiming his agnosticism and ridiculing the message of the Holy Scriptures. As she listened, hope was born in her heart, and she said, 'This is just what I need to deliver me from the slavery of sin!' In following his teaching, she became an intelligent agnostic or infidel. As a result, her whole being revolted against the degradation of the life she had been living. She fled from the den of iniquity where she had been held captive so long and today, rehabilitated, she has won her way back to an honored position in society and is living a clean, virtuous, happy life—all because she is an agnostic.

"Now," he said, addressing the man who had presented him with his card and the challenge, "if you will promise to bring these two people with you as examples of what agnosticism can do, I will promise to meet you at the Academy of Science Hall at four o'clock next Sunday. And I will bring with me at least one hundred men and women who for years lived in the sinful degradation I have tried to depict, but who have been gloriously saved through believing the gospel which you ridicule. I will have these men and women with me on the platform as witnesses to the miraculous saving power of Jesus Christ and as present-day proof of the truth of the Bible."

Ironside then turned to the Salvation Army captain and said, "Captain, have you any who could go with me to such a meeting?"

She exclaimed with enthusiasm, "We can give you forty at least just from this one corps, and we will give you a brass band to lead the procession!"

"Fine," Ironside answered. "Now, sir, I will have no difficulty picking up sixty others from the various missions, gospel halls, and evangelical churches of the city. So if you will promise to bring two such exhibits as I have described, I will come marching in at the head of such a procession, with the band playing 'Onward, Christian Soldiers,' and I will be ready for the debate."

Apparently the man who had made the challenge had some sense of humor, for he smiled wryly and waved his hand in a deprecating kind of way as if to say "Nothing doing!" He then edged out of the crowd while the bystanders applauded Ironside and the other Christian workers.[7]

We have a great treasure in the Scriptures. We should be so convinced of this that we treasure it, read it, study it, and then take it out with courage to present it to a needy generation.

In the 1960s in France, at the same time student riots were erupting on campuses throughout the world, Chinese communist students took over the University of Caen. On a table there, they had spread out some red-bound copies of the thoughts of Mao Tse Tung. They had a banner which said, "Read the little red book by Chairman Mao." The Christian students saw this as a great opportunity. They got in touch with the equivalent of the American Bible Society in France and asked for some red-bound copies of the New Testament. The society sent them. The students then set up their own table in the courtyard and spread out their red-bound New Testaments. A Chinese Christian girl stood behind the table to sell the Testaments. The Christians hung up their banner: "Read the little red book by Jesus Christ."

That is what we have to do—take the book and hold it up before our world and say, This is God's book. It is the hope of the world. It points to Jesus Christ who is the way of salvation. It does so infallibly, and it blesses those who believe it and live by its teaching. Won't you believe it and come to Jesus?[8]

4

Understanding God's Book

I have never felt at ease claiming one verse more than another as my particular life text, as some people do. But if I do have a life text, it is one given to me by the pastor of the church in which I grew up: "Do your best to present yourself to God as one approved, a workman who does not need to be ashamed and who correctly handles the word of truth" (2 Tim. 2:15).

The last phrase of this Scripture particularly interests me. Whether providentially given or not, 2 Timothy 2:15 has characterized much of what I have done in my academic and Christian life. During my grade school and high school years I received

the basic instruction for any young man growing up in an evangelical church. In college I no longer received formal biblical
instruction (at least not in Sunday school), but I supplemented
my earlier knowledge with Christian reading. In seminary I
delved into biblical languages, theology, and church history. I
furthered this study during three years of intensive graduate work
in Switzerland. Since that time I have been engaged in a systematic study and exposition of the Word of God as part of my
responsibilities as pastor of Philadelphia's historic Tenth Presbyterian Church. In spite of what has now become thirty or forty
years of Bible study, I recognize more acutely than ever the danger of handling the Word of God incorrectly.

It is significant, of course, that Paul's encouragement to handle Scripture properly was written to Timothy, the apostle's
young companion to whom Paul was committing general over-
sight of large portions of the early Christian church. Timothy
was no novice. He had known the Holy Scriptures "from
infancy" (2 Tim. 3:15), had had the apostle Paul as his teacher
(2 Tim. 1:13), and had been given a special gift of ministry
"through the laying on of . . . hands" (2 Tim. 1:6). Yet it is precisely to this man that the apostle Paul says, "Present yourself
to God as . . . a workman who. . . correctly handles the word of
truth" (2 Tim. 2:15).

Someone might say, Well, if Timothy had to give special
attention not to treat the Bible incorrectly, effective and accurate study of the Word of God is probably beyond someone like
me. Effective Bible study cannot be done by normal people.
However, such a reaction is precisely the opposite of what the
apostle Paul intended. The Roman Church took this position
in the decrees of the Council of Trent after the beginning of the
Protestant Reformation:

> In order to restrain petulant spirits, it [the Council] decrees that
> no one, relying on his own skill, shall—in matters of faith and
> of morals pertaining to the edification of Christian doctrine—
> wrestling the sacred Scriptures to his own senses, presume to

interpret the said sacred Scripture contrary to that sense which holy mother Church—whose it is to judge of the true sense and interpretation of the holy Scriptures—hath held and doth hold; or even contrary to the unanimous consent of the Fathers; even though such interpretations were never [intended] to be at any time published.[1]

This statement says that only experts—in this case, the fathers of the church—have the right to interpret Scripture. But to this statement the Reformers correctly countered that God has given every Christian the right and power to interpret Scripture for himself. The Reformers did not ignore the danger of distorting Scripture, the matter about which the bishops of Trent were concerned. They replied that the proper way of dealing with this problem was not by entrusting the interpretation of Scripture to some elite body of Christian scholars or theologians, but rather by permitting all Christians to apply proper principles of interpretation to the task of Bible study.

In other words (as the apostle Paul himself also recognized in writing to Timothy) the experts as well as the common Christian can misinterpret. All must handle God's Word carefully and properly. The principles for handling the Bible correctly are for everyone.

Destructive Criticism

Before we develop some guidelines for interpreting the Bible, let us look at some of the erroneous systems of Bible interpretation that have sprung up in recent decades. This preliminary review is valuable for two reasons. First, a look at erroneous systems highlights the proper approach by contrast. Second, since most Christians do not have technical training in the history of biblical interpretation, they should be warned against misleading systems. These include the destructive higher criticism, both in its Old Testament and New Testament forms, and the subjective hermeneutic, which has recently gained great popularity.

The destructive higher criticism began with attacks on the Old Testament and can be dated in its modern form to the middle of the eighteenth century. It is usually associated with the name of Jean Astruc, a scientist and physician who served in the French court. He called attention to a fact that Bible scholars had long noted, namely, that in Genesis God is designated by two different names: Elohim and Jehovah. These are sometimes intermingled freely but there are blocks of Genesis in which only one or the other name is used. Calling attention to this, Astruc proposed that Genesis was actually composed of two or three separate documents, and that the authors had different names for (and even different conceptions of) God.

Astruc's proposal was not yet radical. However, it already had within it those elements soon to be developed fully in succeeding centuries—the so-called "critical method." First, it broke with the traditional views according Moses authorship of Genesis. Second, it shifted attention from the meaning of the text to the supposed sources lying behind the text and to the process by which these various sources assumed their present form. Third, it introduced a new procedure, focusing on the style, vocabulary, syntax, and other features of Genesis as the sole basis upon which its authenticity and integrity could be evaluated.

At first Astruc's work received little notice, but within a few years it was picked up by many German scholars and expanded to include the whole of the Old Testament. Johann Eichhorn applied Astruc's approach to the entire Pentateuch. Wilhelm De Wette and Edouard Reuss attempted to bring the results into line with Jewish history. Reuss concluded that in the correct historical sequence the prophets are earlier than the Law and the Psalms are later than both.

The most popular and, in some sense, the culminating work in this field was the *Prolegomena* of Julius Wellhausen, published in 1878. This work widely disseminated the four-stage documentary hypothesis known as JEPD ("J" for the Jehovah source, "E" for the Elohim source, "P" for the priestly documents and code, and "D" for the later editorial work of the Deuteronomist or Deuteronomic school). It dated the writing of the Law after the Babylonian exile, placing only the Book of the Covenant and the most ancient editing of the "J" and "E" narratives prior to the eighth century B.C.

The profound change this involved is clear in the words of E. C. Blackman, who hailed Wellhausen's achievement as making possible "the understanding of the Old Testament in terms of progressive revelation . . . a real liberation."[2] Emil G. Kraeling noted that it "marked the beginning of a completely secular and evolutionistic study of the Old Testament sources."[3]

In New Testament studies the higher critics directed their energies in a slightly different direction: to recover the Jesus of history through a study of the origins of the gospel narratives and the development of New Testament theology as preserved in the epistles of Paul, the pastorals, the Johannine literature, and Revelation. Yet the same principles were involved and in fact carried forward in an even more radical way in New Testament studies than in the nineteenth-century investigation of the Pentateuch.

The origin of higher critical principles in New Testament study is usually traced to Ferdinand Christian Baur (1792–1860), who organized the material along historical lines. Hegel had developed the view that history proceeds by thesis, antithesis, and synthesis. Baur applied this to biblical history, citing the supposed conflict of Petrine and Pauline theology as evidence of a doctrinal thesis and antithesis within the early church. This led to the synthesis of early Catholicism in Baur's thinking. Although Baur's thesis is rejected today, he succeeded in shaking the traditional views concerning the authorship and composition of the New Testament books—another "liberation"— and called the attention of the scholarly world to a rediscovery of the historical Christ as the primary New Testament problem.

More recently, higher criticism of the New Testament has centered around the work of Rudolf Bultmann, a former professor at the University of Marburg, Germany. Much of Bultmann's energy was expended on stripping away what he felt to be the "mythology" of the New Testament writers—heaven, hell, and miracles. According to Bultmann, what lies beneath the mythology is the church's deepest understanding of life created by its experience with the risen Lord. Consequently, nothing may be known of Jesus in terms of pure history except the mere fact that he existed. In Bultmann's words, "We can know almost nothing concerning the life and personality of Jesus."[4]

Certain characteristics tie together the higher criticism. First, there is humanism. In most forms of the modern debate, the Scriptures of the Old and New Testaments are handled as if they are man's word about God, rather than God's word to man. Within this framework the Bible is only a record of human reflection and action in the field of religion. The interpreter's task becomes the work of sifting that experience and evaluating it for possible use in our age.

The second common characteristic of higher criticism is naturalism, expressed in the belief that the Bible is the result of an evolutionary process. This has been very evident in Old Testament studies in the way the documentary theory of the Pentateuch has developed. But it is also evident in Bultmann's form criticism, for everything depends upon the early church gradually developing its understanding of reality and preserving this at various stages through the written traditions. In this view, early and primitive understandings of God and reality gave way to later, more developed conceptions. From this it follows that the so-called "primitive" ideas may be rejected in favor of more modern ones. Miracles may be discounted. Crude notions such as the wrath of God, sacrifice, a visible second coming of the Lord, and other items may be excluded from the religion of the New Testament.

The third major characteristic of the higher criticism is based upon the first two. It holds that if truth changes, as the evolutionary hypothesis holds, then it continues to change; it has changed since the last books of the Bible were written; and, consequently, we must go beyond the Scriptures to understand true religion.

A Subjective Hermeneutic

The second erroneous approach to biblical interpretation is today's radical subjectivism. This approach does not have a long academic history, as does the destructive higher criticism. In fact, that is its major problem. Subjectivism has no history at all. It is merely the idea—not at all founded on fact or analysis—that Scripture can mean anything, depending upon the thoughts and needs of the one who reads it. We see this view in statements like: Well, that's just your opinion; A person can prove anything from Scripture; or It doesn't matter what you believe as long as reading the Bible, hearing sermons, or going to church help you cope with life.

Unfortunately this view often carries over into the scholarly world, where men and women should at least know better. The task of the scholar is to study documents to see what they really mean and to study important historical periods to learn what really happened and was believed in those periods. But today many seem to think that an objective analysis and single answers are unnecessary.

In *Knowing Scripture,* theologian R. C. Sproul tells of a panel discussion in which he once participated with a group of Bible scholars. The panel discussed a particular New Testament passage, the meaning of which was in dispute. In his opening statement, one of the scholars said, "I think that we should be open and honest about how we approach the New Testament. In the final analysis we all read what we want to read in it, and that's all right."[5]

If this scholar had voiced everything but the last four words, his statement although distressing could at least have been accurate. He would have been saying simply that he and his associates often do misinterpret Scripture. But that is not what he said. He said that he and his associates read into Scripture what they want to find in it and that this is all right! In other words, there is no objective meaning to Scripture. Its only value is subjective, and this may be something for one person and an entirely different something for someone else.

In a system like this, there is no such thing as genuine revelation. There is no sure word from God. Everybody believes what he or she wants to believe. Any valid basis for faith or ethics vanishes. Indeed, even the task of interpretation vanishes, for there is no need or even possibility of handling the word of truth correctly.

Principles for Interpretation

Obviously, we need a proper procedure for interpreting the Bible. We need sound principles. What should they be? Each of the principles suggested here grows out of the nature of the Bible itself. The first ones stem from the Bible as the Word of God. (The fact that the Bible has come through human authors involves other principles that will also be considered.)

Unity and Noncontradiction

First and most important is the truth that the Bible has one author who is God. This leads to two principles of interpretation: first, the principle of unity, and second, the principle of noncontradiction. Taken together they mean that, if the Bible is truly from God, and if God is a God of truth (as he is), then the parts of the book must go together to tell one story. If the parts of the book seem to be in opposition or in contradiction to each other, then our interpretation of one or both of these parts is in error. Likewise, if a scholar expends his efforts highlighting contradictions in the biblical text and does not go on to indicate how they may be resolved, he is not demonstrating his wisdom or honesty as much as he is his failure as an interpreter of the Word of God.

Many claim that trying to find unity where there is no unity is dishonesty. But this is not the case. To argue there is no unity is a matter of interpretation and presupposition.

Take the matter of sacrifices as an example. Everyone recognizes that sacrifices play a large role in the Old Testament while they are not as important in the New Testament. Why? Here one interpreter brings in his idea of an evolving religious conscience. He supposes that sacrifices are important in the most primitive forms of religion and can be explained by the people's fear of the gods or God. God is imagined to be a capricious, vengeful deity. Worshipers try to appease him by sacrifice. Since this seems to be the general idea of sacrifice in the other pagan religions of antiquity, it is assumed for the religion of the ancient Semite peoples too. The interpreter continues to hypothesize that in time this view of God gives way to a more elevated conception. When this happens, God is seen more like a God of justice than a God of capricious whim and wrath. Law begins to take a more prominent place and eventually replaces sacrifice as the center of the religion. The worshipers finally rise to the conception of God as a God of love, and at this point sacrifice disappears entirely. Today this interpreter would regard both sacrifices and the wrath of God as outmoded concepts.

By contrast, another person, perhaps an evangelical, would approach the issue with entirely different presuppositions and would therefore produce an entirely different interpretation. He would begin by noting that the Old Testament does indeed tell a great deal about the wrath of God. But he would add that this element is hardly eliminated as one goes on through the Bible, most certainly not from the New Testament. It is, for instance, an important theme of Paul. It also emerges as a strong theme in the Book of Revelation, where we read of God's just wrath eventually being poured out against the sins of a rebellious and ungodly race.

This is not all, for the idea of sacrifice is also present throughout the Scriptures. It is true that the detailed sacrifices of the Old Testament system are no longer performed in the New Testament churches. But this is not because a supposed primitive conception of God has given way to a more advanced one. Rather it is because the great sacrifice of Jesus Christ has completed and superseded them all, as the Book of Hebrews clearly maintains.

For this interpreter the solution is not found in an evolving conception of God, for God is always the same—a God of wrath toward sin and a God of love toward the sinner. It is found in God's progressing revelation of himself to man, through the sacrifices (with their explicit instructions), intended to teach both the dreadfully serious nature of sin and the way God had always determined to save sinners.

These sacrifices point to Christ. Referring to a phase of Jewish life that all would understand, John the Baptist was able to say, "Look, the Lamb of God, who takes away the sin of the world!" (John 1:29). And Peter could write, "For you know that it was not with perishable things such as silver or gold that you were redeemed from the empty way of life handed down to you from your forefathers, but with the precious blood of Christ, a lamb without blemish or defect" (1 Peter 1:18–19).

While the data is the same, the difference is that one scholar approaches Scripture looking for contradiction and development. The other views it as if God has written it. He therefore looks for unity, allowing one passage of Scripture to throw light on another.

The Analogy of Faith

We now come to a third principle of interpretation, growing out of the truth that God is the Bible's author. This is what the protestant Reformers called "the analogy of faith," meaning that Scripture interprets itself (*Scriptura sui interpres*). The Westminster divines said: "The infallible rule of interpretation of Scripture is the Scripture itself: and therefore, when there is a question about the true and full sense of any Scripture (which is not manifold, by one), it must be searched and known by other places that speak more clearly."[6]

At the International Council on Biblical Inerrancy's Conference on Hermeneutics, meeting in Chicago in the fall of 1982, those who were present declared: "We affirm the unity, harmony, and consistency of Scripture and declare that it is its own best interpreter. We deny that Scripture may be interpreted in such a way as to suggest that one passage corrects or militates against another. We deny that later writers of Scriptures misinterpreted earlier passages of Scripture when quoting from or referring to them" (Article 17).[7]

In simple terms, this means that if a passage of Scripture can be interpreted in two ways, one of which is in harmony with other passages of Scripture and one of which is not, we should choose the interpretation that harmonizes with other texts. This is not dishonest, as some would claim. It is only reasonable, the kind of thing we would readily do even with another human author, not to mention God. If a writer says something in one place that can be interpreted as contradicting what he says in another place, it is only common courtesy to seek an explanation to make the passages consistent. Of course, when dealing with human authors it is possible to find passages that do contradict each other, since human beings are limited in their viewpoints and often err either in the views themselves or in their expressions of them. But this does not hold true for God. If God is the author of the Bible, it is the most reasonable thing in the world to expect his various statements to complement and reinforce each other. If not, God speaks with a forked tongue, and this is unworthy of him.

I do not mean by this that all portions of Scripture are therefore easily understood. Parts of the Bible will always seem difficult to us. However, the difficulties reveal the weakness in our own understanding rather than flaws in God's revelation.

Study the Context

The second great truth about the Bible is that it has been given to us through human channels, even though God is the ultimate source of the Scriptures. This does not mean, as we have seen, that the Bible is subject to error as human books are. It does mean that all sound principles of interpretation must be used in studying the Bible, precisely as they would be used in studying any other document. The way into the mind of God is through the mind of the human author, God's channel. Consequently, the only proper way to interpret the Bible is to discover what these human spokesmen wanted to express.

One necessary part of doing this—a fourth principle—is to consider each biblical statement in context, in this case within the context of the chapter, book, and eventually the entire Word of God. This is an obvious need, since any statement taken out of context can be misleading. But it is something to guard against particularly in the interpretation of the Bible. Frank E. Gaebelein, the author of a very valuable book on interpreting the Bible, says of this error:

> Realizing that the Bible is God's inspired Word, the devout reader attaches peculiar importance to every statement it contains. This reverence is commendable, but when it descends to the practice of picking out single verses as proofs of all sorts of things, it becomes positively dangerous. Were this a sound method of interpretation, one could find biblical support for nearly all the crimes on the calendar, from drunkenness and murder to lying and deceit.[8]

Some people read the Bible at random, dipping here or there. This may be characteristic of the way they do most things in life, but it is a mistake in Bible study. It leads inevitably to the lack of proportion and depth often characteristic of Christian lives today. A far better system is a regular, disciplined study of key books. New Christians could begin with one of the Gospels, perhaps the Gospel of John or Mark. After this they could go on to Acts, Ephesians, Galatians, Romans, or an Old Testament book such as Genesis. It is always valuable to read and meditate on the Psalms as well.

Certain procedures should be followed during each study. First, the book itself should be read through carefully four or five times, perhaps aloud one of these times. Each time something new will strike the reader. Second, the book should be divided into its major sections (not necessarily the same chapters as in our Bibles), just as we divide modern books into chapters, subsections, and paragraphs. At this stage the object is to see what verses belong together, what subjects are covered, and what is the sequence of subjects. Third, these sections should relate to one another: What are the main sections or subjects? Which are introductory? Where are the book's applications? At this stage the reader should be developing an outline of the book and should be able to answer such questions as: What does this book say? To whom was it written? Why was it written? If studying Romans, for example, you should be able to say, This book was written to the church at Rome, but also to churches in all places and at all times. It says that the human race is lost in sin and that the answer to that sin is the righteousness of God revealed in Jesus Christ. Its purpose is to explain this gospel. A minor purpose was to alert the Romans to Paul's desire to visit them on his way to a future ministry in Spain.

The student can now proceed to a more detailed study of individual sections: What is the main subject of each section? What is said about it? Why is it said? What are the conclusions?

Alongside serious, in-depth study of one book or section, the student should also attempt to become acquainted with the whole Bible. This means reading it comprehensively. Naturally, many parts of the Bible will not appeal to us at first. But if we never become acquainted with them, we limit our growth and may even warp our understanding. Paul told Timothy, "*All* scripture is God-breathed and is useful for teaching, rebuking, correcting and training in righteousness" (2 Tim. 3:16, *emphasis mine*).

Consider the Style

A fifth principle is to consider the style of the material and then interpret it within that framework. This is obviously a need when dealing with poetical literature such as Psalms, Proverbs, Job, and even parts of the prophetic material. Poetic books frequently employ symbols or images and are misinterpreted if taken literally.

The Book of Revelation should not be taken literally in all its parts. Take the example of the vision of Jesus found in the opening verses. Such an interpretation results in a monstrosity—a figure entirely white, having hair like wool, eyes like fire, feet like heated and glowing bronze, a sword going out of his mouth, and seven stars in his right hand. However, when each of these items is discovered to be an image associated with God in the Old Testament, then the vision yields a portrait of Jesus, shown to be one with God the Father in all his attributes. He is the holy, eternal, omniscient, omnipresent, revealing, and sovereign God.

Style also has a bearing on the Lord's use of parables—a special method of teaching. Usually a parable makes one or, at best, a few main points. Consequently, it is wrong to fix an application to each detail of the story. For example, an attempt to assign a meaning to the husks, pigs, and other details of the story of the prodigal son is simply ludicrous.

Historical Versus Didactic Material

A sixth principle of interpretation is to interpret historical material by didactic material. Historical material is narration, the accounts of what happened in the past. Didactic material is teaching material. It is important for the didactic material to interpret the historical material rather than the other way around. Things that happened in history are sometimes right and sometimes wrong, sometimes normative and sometimes extraordinary. If we use historical material to determine what we should believe or do now, we are often misled.

Consider the example of the coming of the Holy Spirit at Pentecost, an extraordinary event prophesied in the Old Testament (Acts 2:14–26). Speaking on that occasion, Peter called attention to its being a fulfillment of Joel 2:28–32. There was a sound like the blowing of a violent wind at Pentecost. The disciples saw tongues of fire that separated and rested on each of them. They were able to speak in other languages by the power of the Holy Spirit.

On the basis of this account, some people argue that the same three effects of wind, fire, and tongues should be present whenever any person is "filled" with or "baptized" by the Holy Spirit, or at least he or she should be able to speak in tongues! Surely this is a misuse of historical narration. It may be the case that some who receive the Holy Spirit speak in tongues, but the fact that this happened on one occasion and may happen on other occasions does not mean that it is normative or even desirable for all Christians. Indeed, even in the Book of Acts this does not seem to have been the universal experience of believers.

A doctrine of the Holy Spirit ought to be drawn from the teaching passages of the Bible. The discourses in the latter half of John's Gospel are examples of such passages. Galatians 5:22–23, which describes the fruit of the Spirit as "love, joy, peace, patience, kindness, goodness, faithfulness, gentleness and self-control" is another example. These passages are normative. Others are only records of past happenings.

Why Was It Written?

A seventh principle is to consider the purpose for which a particular passage was written. Most passages deal with spiritual things, primarily with what it means to be and live as a child of God. A passage is very seldom (perhaps never) written to give modern scientific explanations of the universe.

One obvious application of this principle is to those references that bothered Rudolf Bultmann so much, in which heaven is assumed to be "up there" and hell "below" our feet. It also applies to passages saying that bones cry out, bowels yearn, kidneys instruct, and ears judge. Some maintain that these references reveal a mistaken notion of the universe and the human constitution, but this is absurd. What these passages demonstrate is that biblical writers wrote in the idiom of their day so they would be understood. Their use of such phrases was no more a mistake than our use of such phrases as "walking on air," a "gut feeling," and "deep in my heart."

Because it is not always easy to determine whether a passage is using literal or figurative language, care must be taken. Most importantly, however, one should be aware of the problem and seek consciously for the true scope of the passage.

The Meaning of Words

Another need flowing from the Bible as both human and divine—an eighth principle—is to give attention to the meaning of words. Although it is possible for God to think without words, it is certain we cannot. Thoughts cannot be expressed without words. Consequently, the meanings of words and an individual's use of them are of great importance. In studying words, we must be aware that meanings change over time, even within the scope of the Bible itself. One is often helped in this type of study by such works as Gerhardt Kittel's *Theological Dictionary of the New Testament* (nine volumes), or by other dictionaries and study aids.

Suppose you are studying Romans 3:21–26 and want to learn more about the important word *righteousness*. One key verse is 10:3, in which the righteousness of God is distinguished from our righteousness. Romans 1:17 says that the righteousness of God is made known in the gospel. In all, the word *righteousness* is used thirty-five times in this one letter. Most of these uses throw light on other uses. You will also observe the use of the word in other books of the Bible, perhaps by using the chain reference system in some Bibles. Dictionaries contain the derivations of words and will throw light on their meanings as well.

When we are using an older version of the Bible, such as the Authorized or King James Version, we should also remember that sometimes the words have shifted meanings. For example, the King James Version of 1 Thessalonians 4:15 says: "We which are alive and remain unto the coming of the Lord shall not prevent them which are asleep." According to modern English usage, *prevent* means that those who are alive at Christ's return will not be able to stop those who have died from also rising to be with him. But that is not the meaning. At the time of the King James translation prevent meant "precede" or "come before" (from the Latin root *prae venire*). The text really means that the dead in Christ shall rise first and the living shall then accompany them into Christ's presence.

The summary of these points is contained in what has come to be called the historical-literal or grammatical-literal method of biblical interpretation. This simply means, as J. I. Packer puts it, that "the proper, natural sense of each passage (i.e., the intended sense of the writer) is to be taken as fundamental."[9] The intended meaning of the words in their own context and in the speech of the original writer or spokesman is the starting point.

> In other words, Scripture statements must be interpreted in the light of the rules of grammar and discourse on the one hand, and of their own place in history on the other. This is what we should expect in the nature of the case, seeing that the biblical books originated as occasional documents addressed to contemporary audiences; and it is exemplified in the New Testament exposition of the Old, from which the fanciful allegorizing practiced by Philo and the Rabbis is strikingly absent.[10]

This principle is based on the fact that the Bible is God's Word in man's language. It means that Scripture should be interpreted in its natural sense, and theological or cultural preferences must not be allowed to obscure this fundamental meaning.

Obeying God's Word

The Bible has been given by God to provoke a personal response in us. If we do not respond to it, we inevitably misuse it (even in studying it) and misinterpret it. One example of this occurs when Jesus said to the Jewish leaders, "You diligently study the Scriptures because you think that by them you possess eternal life. These are the Scriptures that testify about me, yet you refuse to come to me to have life. I do not accept praise from men, but I know you. I know that you do not have the love of God in your hearts. . . . How can you believe if you accept praise from one another, yet make no effort to obtain the praise that comes from the only God?" (John 5:39–42, 44).

No one could fault the Jews of Christ's day for having a low opinion of the Scriptures—they actually had the highest regard for them. Nor could they be faulted for a lack of meticulous study—the Jews did study the Scriptures and in fact prized them. But in their high regard for Scripture, they quite easily passed over its intention. Their lives were not changed. Although they gained honor from men for their detailed knowledge of it, they did not gain salvation.

Later in John's Gospel we find another example of this. In chapter 9 John told the story of the healing of a man who had been born blind. He was physically blind, of course. But the meat of the story lies in the fact he was also spiritually blind before Christ touched him. Afterward he came to spiritual sight. When the man was healed he came into conflict with the Jewish rulers. They knew about Jesus, but they did not believe in him. They did not believe because of their attitude toward the Scriptures. For them the revelation recorded in the Old Testament was an end in itself. Nothing could be added, and nothing was required. They said, "We know that God spoke to Moses, but as for this fellow, we don't even know where he comes from" (v. 29). The man who had once been blind did not compete with them in their acknowledged mastery of the Old Testament. Instead he pointed to the fact of his healing when he concluded, "If this man were not from God, he could do nothing" (v. 33). In treating the Old Testament as an end in itself, the Jews actually perverted it and missed its true meaning. They failed to see that the Old Testament law, coming through Moses, testified precisely to Jesus.

In its simplest form, this means we must obey the Bible if we are to understand it in the fullest sense. This is a ninth principle of interpretation. We can understand the Bible superficially (enough to know what it is we are refusing to obey), but God hides the deep things of his Word from any who are unwilling to obey him.

Jesus told us we will only know the truth about him if we are willing to do his will, that is, if we allow ourselves to be changed by the truths we find in Scripture. He said, "If any one chooses to do God's will [that is, if he determines to do it], he will find out whether my teaching comes from God or whether I speak on my own" (John 7:17). We must not assume we will be able fully to understand any passage of Scripture unless we are willing to be changed by it.

Waiting on God

A final principle springs from the internal witness of the Spirit to the truth of God's Word. Here Scripture speaks succinctly. The Holy Spirit was active in the writing of the biblical books. He is active also in conveying the truth of the Bible to the minds of those who read it. Paul wrote to the Corinthians: "We have not received the spirit of the world but the Spirit who is from God, that we may understand what God has freely given us. This is what we speak, not in words taught us by human wisdom but in words taught by the Spirit, expressing spiritual truths in spiritual words" (1 Cor. 2:12–13). The Bible deals with spiritual themes, and we need the activity of the Holy Spirit to understand them. The Holy Spirit is the teacher of Christians. Moreover, he brings forth new life in those who hear the gospel.

So the tenth principle is we must pray as we study the Scriptures, asking the Holy Spirit to enlighten us. The Spirit's presence is not given to us to make a careful and diligent study of the Word of God unnecessary but rather to make it effective. Prayer solves the problem of studying the Bible for its own sake, as we discussed earlier. By prayer we avoid the formalism of the scribes. In true Bible study we first ask the Holy Spirit to open our minds to understanding his truths, and then we obey the truths as he applies them to our lives.

The author of Psalm 119 indicated the proper attitude when he wrote,

> Do good to your servant, and I will live;
> I will obey your word.
> Open my eyes that I may see
> wonderful things in your law.
>
> Psalm 119:17–18

What does a prayer like this accomplish? It makes us conscious we are meeting God in our reading and not merely going through some prescribed religious ritual. After we pray we must say to ourselves, God is now going to speak to me, and then we must read to hear what he says. There is probably nothing more exciting than this—to know that as we read, God is actually speaking to us personally and teaching us! This makes Bible study and its accompanying prayer a time of personal communion with him.[11]

Here is a summary of the ten principles of sound Bible interpretation:

Principles Growing Out of the Fact That God Is the Bible's Author

1. *The principle of unity.* Since the Bible has one author, namely God, the parts of the Bible must go together to form one overall story, and they must present one consistent theology. If they do not seem to do this, we are misinterpreting.
2. *The principle of noncontradiction.* Since the Bible has one author, one section of the Bible will not truly oppose or contradict another.

3. *The principle of the analogy of faith.* The best interpreter of Scripture is Scripture itself. Less obscure passages will throw light on more obscure ones.
4. *The principle of context.* Biblical statements are not unrelated oracles; therefore, they are not to be torn away. They must be interpreted within the context of the chapter, book, and eventually, the entire Word of God.

Principles Growing Out of the Fact That
the Bible Also Has Human Authors

5. *The principle of style.* The style of a passage must be taken into consideration. Poetry must be considered as poetry, parables as parables, historical material as historical material, and so on.
6. *The principle of didactic material interpreting historical material.* Historical happenings are sometimes right and sometimes wrong, sometimes normal and sometimes abnormal. Teaching material shows how historical material is to be interpreted.
7. *The principle of purpose.* The chief end or purpose of the writing of a passage should govern our interpretation. A passage cannot be used to teach what it was not written to teach.
8. *The principle of the importance of words.* Thoughts cannot be conveyed without words. It is therefore important to study words and know their exact (and sometimes changing) meanings.

A Principle Growing Out of the Fact That
God Has Given Us the Bible for a Spiritual Purpose

9. *The principle of obedience.* The deep things of the Bible are hidden from those who refuse to obey its teachings.

A Principle Growing Out of the Fact That
We Need the Help of the Holy Spirit to
Understand the Bible Correctly

10. *The principle of prayer.* It is easy to err in interpreting any document, especially when we are dealing with one presenting spiritual matters. We must ask God to send his Holy Spirit to guide our understanding. The Holy Spirit is given not to make careful, disciplined study of the Word of God unnecessary but rather to make it effective.

5

ALLEGED PROBLEMS IN THE BIBLE

I was taught a Sunday school lesson years ago entitled "God's Problem." It presented the holiness and justice of God, emphasizing that God cannot excuse the guilty. It presented the love of God, stressing that God wants to save sinners. Then it proposed this difficulty: How can a God who must act justly save the sinner he loves? This was put forward as a great problem for God. The solution was then offered in terms of Christ's atonement.

We can understand why a lesson might be presented this way—it condescends to human ways of thinking. Yet when we think about it, we realize God did not really have a problem when it came to deciding how he was going to save our fallen race. To imagine God with such a problem is to think of God sitting on the ramparts of heaven, looking down on sinful humanity, and wringing his hands, saying, How in the world am I going to save these poor people whom I love? As he scratches his head, a light suddenly goes on, and God says, I know what I'll do! I'll send my Son to die.

Certainly nothing of that sort ever happened. Jesus was the Lamb slain before the foundation of the world. God was never confused. He never searched for answers. The only real problem is the problem arising in our own minds as we contemplate what seems to us to be a difficulty.

When we talk about problems in the Bible, we have a similar situation. Actually, there are no problems in the Bible. God is a God of perfection. The Bible is God's Word. Therefore, it is as true and perfect as God himself. If there are problems with our way of thinking, this is because we aren't thinking properly, not because of what God has done.

Point of Departure

When I went to seminary I firmly believed the Scriptures were the Word of God and therefore inerrant. Nevertheless, when confronted by the views of unbelieving men able to produce data that made my own views look foolish, I had to decide what to do. I wrestled with this. When I got through sorting it out, the most helpful thing for me was to recognize that the problems were in me, not in the Word of God, and that I could solve most of them if I would simply approach the Word on that basis.

If you begin with the assumption the Bible is full of contradictions, you are going to find contradictions. Although they will not be real contradictions, your bias will make them seem like contradictions. On the other hand, if you approach the Bible believing it is the Word of God and that Scripture is its own best interpreter (the great principle of the Reformation studied in the last chapter) then, much to your surprise, you will discover the many things wise and influential men have said to be problems actually aren't problems at all.

A pastor from Canada sent me a letter listing a number of Bible difficulties. From the tone of the letter I could not tell whether he was presenting these to refute the Bible's inerrancy or simply as things he did not understand. I assumed the latter and began to work through some of the items he had listed. In almost every case his difficulties were solved simply by reading the Scriptures carefully.

The pastor included a paragraph about the various accounts of the ascension of Jesus as we find them in the Gospels. He pointed out that Matthew and John omit reference to the Ascension entirely. He considered this a problem. Then he argued that there was a contradiction between Acts 1:3 where Jesus was with the disciples forty days between the Resurrection and the Ascension, and Mark and Luke's inference that Jesus ascended to heaven very shortly, perhaps one or two days, after his resurrection. I pointed out to him that careful reading of the passages would illuminate their meaning.

Acts says explicitly that forty days passed between the Resurrection and the Ascension. However, it is not true that Mark and Luke say that Jesus ascended a day or two after the Resurrection. In fact, in reading Mark carefully, you discover Mark contains several words or phrases indicating an undetermined amount of time had passed. For example, in verse 12 of the last chapter Mark used the word "afterward," that is, "after these things." In verse 14 he said, "Later Jesus appeared to the Eleven." Then, in verse 19, he wrote, "After the Lord Jesus had spoken." Here we have three indications of a passage of time.

The same thing is true of Luke's account. It would be strange indeed if in his Gospel, Luke said Jesus ascended a day or two after the Resurrection and then in the Book of Acts wrote that he ascended forty days later. In such a case we would give most people the benefit of the doubt and assume we had misunderstood them. Why should we not do the same with biblical authors?

The Canadian pastor also called attention to the thieves who were crucified with Jesus. Again he made the point that John does not tell the story, which is true. But this means nothing. Silence is not necessarily a contradiction. Then the pastor pointed out that Matthew and Mark write about the thieves (plural) cursing Jesus, while Luke says one thief cursed him while the other turned to Jesus and said, "Jesus, remember me when you come into your kingdom" (Luke 23:42). On the surface this presents a dilemma. But it is very easy to resolve the problem. Presumably both thieves cursed Jesus at first. Nothing would be more natural. But one thief, being overcome by the silent endurance and winning character of Christ, began to quiet down and search his own heart. As the Holy Spirit brought repentance, this man turned to the Lord and said, "Remember me when you come into your kingdom." This is the way most commentators have interpreted these seemingly contradictory statements. There is no reason they should not.

One day nearly ten years after receiving this letter I was leaving to speak to a group of men on this very subject and stopped to look at my mail. There I found another letter from this pastor. I opened it and was startled to find a listing of the very problems he had raised with me a decade earlier! Apparently, the answers had made not the slightest impression on him. He had been too narrowly predisposed toward finding these contradictions.

The majority of things brought forward as grave, overwhelming problems or great, unresolvable contradictions can be solved quite simply if we approach the Bible recognizing that we are the ones with the problem, not the Bible.

One of the areas often addressed in question-and-answer sessions during my International Council on Biblical Inerrancy (ICBI) years was how I explain the apparent contradiction between Genesis 15:13 and Exodus 12:41. These two verses refer to the number of years the Israelites are said to have been in Egypt. Genesis uses the figure 400. Exodus says the years were 430. Stephen in his sermon in the Book of Acts uses the 430-year period. Are these contradictions?

I wrote for the ICBI, "That's not a great problem. It is probably the case that the two writers simply start at a different period
when they begin to number the years, or the one is rounding the
figure off." However, a pastor of a Baptist church in Iowa wrote to
me in reply, "You just didn't read the text carefully enough. It's all
very clear if you read it carefully." He pointed out that Genesis
15:13 reads, "They [the Jews] will be enslaved and mistreated 400
years." But Exodus 12:41 says, "Now the length of time the Israelite
people lived in Egypt was 430 years." The Jews lived in Egypt 430
years, but they were not enslaved for the entire period. Under
Joseph they enjoyed a period of prosperity.

The second thing I have found to be helpful in dealing with
Bible difficulties is to divide them into categories. People who
maintain the Bible is full of errors have a tendency to add, This
is an error and this and this and this, thereby jumbling up a number of unrelated things. It is helpful to stop, sort them out, and
think through them one at a time.

Let me suggest a number of categories and discuss how we
should deal with the most common problems in each.

Moral Problems

The first category contains moral problems. Assuming God is
a God of love, how could he command or even allow some of the
things we find in the pages of his Word? One of the most common examples given is God's command to the Israelites to kill
the Canaanites—old, young, men, women, children—blot them
off the face of the earth. People ask, How could a loving God do
this? How could he direct his people to slaughter an innocent
nation? Right there is our error. Innocent? The Canaanites were
not innocent. They were far from innocent.

But what about the issue of the suffering of the righteous? We
may agree that the Canaanites were not innocent, but what
about the righteous? This is a legitimate difficulty arising frequently in Scripture. You find it in the prophets. Joel witnessed
a great locust invasion and asked, "Where does this come from?

Why does it come? Why is this happening to the people of God?"
Habakkuk recognized the sin of his people, yet he knew God
was sending an ungodly nation to conquer them. The prophet
asked how God could allow them to be conquered by a people
who were less righteous than they. The problem appears also in
Job, whom God considered a righteous man. God said to Satan,
"Have you considered my servant Job? There is no one on earth
like him; he is blameless and upright, a man who fears God and
shuns evil" (Job 1:8). Yet Job was allowed to suffer great things:
the loss of possessions, family, and eventually even his health.
How can a loving God permit these things?

Part of the answer is that God has a purpose even if we do not
see it. That is really what the Book of Job is about. Job wanted
an answer to the problem of the suffering of the righteous. The
answer is that a struggle was unfolding on two levels: a heavenly
level (what was happening between God and Satan, which Job
could not see) and an earthly level. Job could not understand
what was going on. But he said, in effect, "There must be more
to this than I see, I just don't understand it." He was willing to
leave his terrible problems with God.

Another answer to the problem of suffering is much, much
harder for us to receive, though it is also more profound. Whenever we talk about evil things happening to the righteous, we
are looking from a human point of view, and we are actually asking the wrong question. What we are asking is, Why did God
let that happen to him or her? The question should be, Why
doesn't God let it happen to us all?

The Lord dealt with this issue in two incidents recorded in
Luke 13:1–5. Some people had pointed to a recent tragedy:
Herod's soldiers had slaughtered a group of Galileans who were
offering sacrifices at the temple. These were devout men and
women in the very act of worship. There was also the matter of
the tower of Siloam that fell over and killed many innocent people. If God is all-powerful and can do as he wants, and if he is
loving and therefore cares about us, how can situations like these

occur? Either God is not all-powerful and could not have prevented them, or he is not all-loving and does not care.

Jesus replied, "Do you think that these Galileans were worse sinners than all the other Galileans because they suffered this way? I tell you, no! But unless you repent, you too will all perish. Or those eighteen who died when the tower of Siloam fell on them—do you think they were more guilty than all the others living in Jerusalem? I tell you, no! But unless you repent, you too will all perish." Jesus was telling them that asking a moral question of God such as, God, how can you let this happen in your universe? places us on very dangerous ground because we are asking the wrong question. The real question should be, God, why hasn't it happened to me? Why am I still living, sinner that I am? Why am I not in hell this very minute?

Scientific Problems

The second category of alleged problems includes questions about science. These fall into a number of different categories themselves. People argue, The Bible talks about the sun rising, but we know that the sun doesn't rise. It only appears to rise because the earth is turning. The Bible is in error when it talks about a sunrise. Or again, Jesus called the mustard seed the smallest of all seeds. But we know today that the mustard seed is not the smallest of all seeds. There are smaller seeds. Or they read the account of the construction of the laver in front of the temple of Solomon and note it was ten cubits across and thirty cubits around. That would make π, the figure by which one calculates the circumference of a circle, to be 3. But π is not 3. It is 3.1416. The Bible is wrong when it speaks in those terms. (Actually when we insist on the Bible being accurate at this point we are being hypocritical. While it is true that π is not 3, it is also not 3.1416. It is 3.14159265 ad infinitum. The decimal point goes on and on, because π is a figure with no end.)

When describing the sun's rising, the Bible writer is using phenomenal language, that is, looking at things as they appear rather than as they are. The author describes the sun as rising and setting because from our point of view that is what it seems to do. We do the same! I doubt very much if any scientist who wakes up early and sees a beautiful scene out in the eastern sky, says, Look at the beautiful effect that is achieved by the earth rotating on its axis, giving us the appearance of the sun rising over the horizon. Like anybody else, he exclaims, "Look at the beautiful sunrise!" His words are not error, and neither are the words of the Bible when it uses such figurative language.

In the example of the mustard seed, the Bible is referring to common experience. When Jesus said, "The mustard seed is the smallest of all seeds," he was not saying, With my expert knowledge of the size of all the seeds in the world, I can tell you the mustard seed is in fact the smallest. He was simply saying, Of the seeds you are familiar with, the mustard seed is the smallest, and I want to use that for an illustration. It is a statement based on common experience. It should not be taken any other way.

Finally, there is the case of the laver. In *The Battle for the Bible* Harold Lindsell works out the solution. He notes that the laver was a handbreadth in thickness (1 Kings 7:26), that is, about four inches. He assumes the diameter measurement was from outside rim to outside rim while the circumference measurement was around the inside. By subtracting eight inches (2 x 4) from 180 inches (10 cubits) you get 172, and 172 divided into 580 (30 cubits) gives 3.14.[1] While that may be an answer, it seems artificial to me. I think the 10 and 30 cubits are simply general statements. After all, we are not even sure the laver was perfectly round, since it was obviously not milled on a machine.

Another scientific problem is the matter of miracles. When the Bible says the sun stood still, that is probably a miracle. I recognize this might be phenomenal language, too. God might have done something we do not understand to have given the appearance that the sun stood still. Some would say that is the preferable explanation. On the other hand, it is possible God could actually have stopped the earth's rotation. This is hard for us to understand because we know the difficulties. If you are driving along in a car at sixty miles an hour and you suddenly slam on the brakes, you fall forward. We assume that if the earth suddenly stopped, everybody would fall over. But God is certainly up to the miracle. And whether this can be explained by appeal to pure miracle or not, there are incidents in the Bible that are certainly miracles and that cannot be escaped by rationalistic explanations.

The resurrection of Jesus Christ was the greatest miracle of all. If God could do that, he could handle the other things as well. We should not be obscurantists at this point. We should not stop working out scientific difficulties if we can. But sometimes when it gets to the bottom line, we simply have to say that our God is a God of miracles, and we must stand with the teaching of the Bible that miracles do occur.

Historical Problems

Some scholars argue that the Bible communicates as history facts we know are not true. Does it? In this particular category of alleged error, time has shown itself to be on the Bible's side. That is, as the evidence of archaeology, history, word studies, and all the things that go into a detailed scientific study of the Old and New Testaments comes in, these problems tend to be resolved.

Second Kings 15:29 refers to a king of Assyria named Tiglath-Pileser. He is said to have conquered the Israelites of the Northern Kingdom and to have taken many of them into captivity. A generation ago liberal scholars were saying that this king never existed and that the account of the fall of Israel to Assyria was mythology. The reason for this was they had no evidence this king ever existed apart from this statement in the Bible. However, archaeologists eventually excavated Tiglath-Pileser's capital city and found his name pressed into bricks which read: "I, Tiglath-Pileser, king of Assyria . . . am a conqueror (of the regions) from the Great Sea which is in the country of Amurru as far as the Great Sea which is in the Nairi country," that is, the Mediterranean.[2] In other words, archaeologists have found testimony, not only to Tiglath-Pileser's existence, but also to the fact that he had pushed his kingdom westward as far as the Mediterranean and had therefore conquered the Northern Kingdom of Israel, as the Bible says he did. The English reader can find accounts of his battles in James B. Pritchard's *Ancient Near Eastern Texts Relating to the Old Testament*, from which the quote above is taken.

As another example, a generation ago scholars were saying Moses could not have written the Pentateuch, the first five books of the Old Testament, because, so the argument went, writing was not known in Moses' day. That seems irrefutable. If nobody knew how to write in Moses' day, Moses obviously did not know how to write; and if Moses did not know how to write, he obviously did not write the Pentateuch. It is not the logic that is wrong in this case, it is the premise, the starting point. As scholars have worked in the area of the Near East, they have discovered people did know how to write in Moses' day. Furthermore, not only did they know how to write, there were actually many written languages. We now know of at least six different languages from the very area of the world in which Moses led the people during the years of wandering.

More recently scholars have denied the reliability of the historical books of the New Testament because they were not written close enough to the time of the events they describe. The synoptic Gospels (Matthew, Mark, and Luke) were dated late, and John, with the greatest measure of Greek flavoring, was pushed into the second Christian century (and by more radical scholars, even into the third). Then, a piece of papyrus was uncovered with several verses of John 18 written on it. It was found in the wrapping of a mummy whose embalming was placed no later than A.D. 125, or perhaps earlier. This authenticated the date of the original writing as within the first century and thus within the lifetime of the apostle John, who has traditionally been identified as the writer.

The results of scientific research, far from discrediting the Bible, are actually supporting its truthfulness. Of course, they do not prove inerrancy—we will probably never have all the data necessary to do that. But they do point in the direction of reliability and reveal nothing that is not compatible with the highest view of Scripture.

A visual illustration might explain the Bible's reliability. Imagine a line going from left to right, from point A to point B, that represents all the data in the Bible. Now divide this line into two parts. One part is a solid line, representing all the solid data, the data we have no reason for doubting. The second part of the line is dotted, representing data with some questions. Now, which of the two parts is longer, the solid line or the dotted line? Any honest scholar, liberal or conservative, would answer that when dealing with the historical data of the Bible, the solid line is longer. (There might be some difference about how much longer. Someone might make the solid line 80 percent of the whole. Someone else might make it 90 percent. But all would admit that the Bible is a very reliable book.)

Now, as the data has been coming in over the last decades, in what direction is the solid line moving? Do we find more problems, making the dotted line get longer and longer and the solid line get shorter and shorter? Or does the solid line get longer and the dotted line shorter? I am convinced that any honest scholar—whether liberal, conservative, or whatever—would testify that as the data comes in, the solid line gets longer and the dotted line gets shorter. In other words, the Bible is increasingly vindicated. Since that is the case, it is not obscurantism on our part when we come up against a difficulty without an immediate answer, simply to say, "I'm going to postpone judgment in that area while more data comes in, because the data tends to support the historicity of the narrative."

When I am speaking to students, particularly seminarians, I sometimes say, "If you want to get a reputation for being very wise today and are willing to risk looking like a fool twenty years from now, point out the errors in the Bible. But if, like Charles Haddon Spurgeon, you are willing to be thought a fool now, knowing that in twenty or thirty years your position will be vindicated, then take your stand on the inerrancy of this book."

In December, 1974, *Time* magazine ran a cover story entitled "How True Is the Bible?" I was fascinated with this article, because I wanted to see what a secular magazine would do with that question. In my judgment, it did a very good job. The writers analyzed the trends, talking about the liberal and conservative positions, and then in a rather balanced way concluded:

> The breadth, sophistication and diversity of all this biblical investigation are impressive, but it begs a question: Has it made the Bible more credible or less? Literalists who feel the ground move when a verse is challenged would have to say that credibility has suffered. Doubt has been sown, faith is in jeopardy. But believers who expect something else from the Bible may well conclude that its credibility has been enhanced. After more than two centuries of facing the heaviest scientific guns that could be brought to bear, the Bible has survived—and is perhaps the better for the siege. Even on the critics' own terms—historical fact—the Scriptures seem more acceptable now than they did when the rationalists began the attack.[3]

Time is not an evangelical magazine, of course, but that is not a bad statement for a secular magazine. At any rate, after I read that I said to myself, "I'm going to wait two weeks and see the letters to the editor, because I'll bet there are some strong reactions to this." Sure enough, in the January 13, 1975, issue, two letters appeared. One was from Martin Marty, a professor at the University of Chicago and a regular writer for the *Christian Century*. The other was from Harvey Cox of the Harvard Divinity School. *Time* usually prints short letters of three to ten lines. These took up a column and a half. The first began, "The faith of your Bible believers is the opposite of biblical faith." When I read that I got angry. I thought that was terribly unfair. *Time* had presented a balanced article. It hadn't claimed inerrancy, simply credibility. These men could not stand even to have the Bible called credible! I got so angry I had to stop and pray. Then, although I did not hear a voice from heaven, I think the Lord said, Don't worry about it. It's not bothering me. Why should it bother you? Just go on and read the magazine.

So I did. The letters were on page 38. I read to page 65 where I discovered why God had told me to go on reading. On that page in the science section was a report of an archaeological expedition in Palestine under the direction of a Jewish archaeologist named Beno Rothenberg. This man had excavated in the southern area of the Sinai in a region known as Solomon's Mines. He wanted to discover the origins of the mining and smelting operations conducted there. His conclusion? The area had been worked by Solomon and his people and before that by the Egyptians, but that neither had started them. The Egyptians had borrowed their metallurgical techniques from the Midianites. Being aware that few of its readers would know who the Midianites were, *Time* put in the following explanation: " . . . the Midianites, a little-known people who dwelled in the area and are identified in Genesis as the first metal workers."[4]

When I got to that point I said, "Holy Spirit, you really do have a sense of humor." Of all the places that particular story could have appeared, it appeared in the very issue in which the liberal scholars were saying, "The faith of your Bible believers is the opposite of biblical faith." This is what I mean by data continuing to come in.

Inconsistencies

The last category of Bible problems is what I call internal inconsistencies. Sometimes following my talks about the Bible's supposed historical errors—the existence of Tiglath-Pileser, writing in Moses' time, dating the fourth Gospel—liberal scholars have come up to me and said, "It's not fair of you to talk along those lines, because you're going back into the past. In dipping into the past, evangelicals have said some rather foolish things, too. Our errors were simply mistakes, and we wish you'd give them up." My reply has been that if one wants to talk about historical difficulties, one has to go back into the past, because the scholars are not proposing such problems today. The reason they are not is precisely what I have been pointing out, that as the data has come in, these problems have tended to explode in their faces.

If liberal scholars are not discussing alleged historical errors today, what are they talking about? This is very interesting. In reading their literature, you find they have almost entirely abandoned the approaches I have mentioned—moral problems, scientific problems, historical problems—and have instead fallen back on their last line of defense, supposed inconsistencies in the Bible itself.

We have two good examples from fairly recent times. One is an article by William LaSor, a professor at Fuller Theological Seminary, in the seminary publication *Theology News and Notes*, in which he presents nine such difficulties.[5] The other is a chapter of a book by Dewey M. Beegle entitled *Scripture, Tradition and Infallibility*, in which he presents eleven.[6] I am not going to discuss those here. It would make this chapter too long and Gleason L. Archer, professor of Old Testament at Trinity Evangelical Divinity School, has already answered them in a paper entitled, "Alleged Errors and Discrepancies in the Original Manuscripts of the Bible."[7] Anybody interested in these problems can read the literature.

Let's look at another inconsistency problem. In John 19:14, John speaks about the moment Pilate gave his verdict condemning Jesus as "the sixth hour." The Synoptics apparently fix it earlier, Mark in particular saying that it was "the third hour" when they crucified him (Mark 15:25). In ancient times hours were usually reckoned from sunrise. John seems to be saying Jesus was condemned around noon (six hours after a 6:00 A.M. sunrise), while Mark is writing he had been condemned and was actually on the cross by 9:00 A.M.

One way to solve this dilemma is to suggest that John is reckoning time not by Jewish, but by Roman standards, which computes from midnight. If this is so, John's reference is to 6:00 A.M.

rather than noon. But this does not really solve the problem. In the first place it is questionable whether the Romans actually reckoned time this way. Leon Morris and others believe they did so only in legal documents. Even if they did, and even if John is adopting their system, there is still a difference of three hours between John and Mark.

Moreover, it is difficult to see how the events recorded by the various Gospels can be packed into so short a time span. Assuming that the Sanhedrin began their official trial at dawn or even slightly before dawn, it was still necessary for Christ to appear before Pilate, the discussion and choice regarding Barabbas to be made, the scourging and then a final interrogation by Pilate. Could all this have taken place by 6:00 A.M. or even before 9:00 A.M.? It is doubtful. We are closer to the truth if we surmise the greater part of the morning hours to be filled with such things.

Does this mean that Mark is wrong? Not necessarily. In the first place we must recognize that no one in antiquity had watches and therefore time was always reckoned in general categories. The day as a whole was divided, like the night, into four portions of three hours each. The night periods were designated as the four watches. The day periods were referred to generally by the first hour of each period: the first hour, the third hour, the sixth hour, and the ninth hour respectively. This explains why the New Testament hardly ever mentions any hour save the third, sixth, and ninth, and it also explains why the expressions "nearly" or "about" are so frequent.

Bearing these facts in mind, we may deduce that Mark and the other synoptic Gospels indicate that Jesus was crucified during that period of the day designated as "the third hour," that is, between the hours of 9:00 A.M. and noon. On the other hand John, who says "about the sixth hour," indicates that it was in fact getting on toward midday when the trial before Pilate was completed.

A final example of inconsistencies concerns the genealogies of Christ. It does not require a great New Testament scholar or even an astute reader of the New Testament to recognize that,

when we read the genealogy as Matthew gives it and contrast it
with the genealogy written by Luke, we are dealing at least in
portions with two entirely different things. This would be all
right if we were dealing with the descent of two different people. But these genealogies both mention Joseph, the husband of
Mary the mother of Jesus, and they are different in listing the
ancestors between Joseph and David. Luke traces Joseph's
descendants to David through Nathan, one of David's sons, while
Matthew traces what is apparently the same line of descent
through Solomon, another of David's sons. Luke says that Joseph
was the son of Heli (3:23), but Matthew says that Joseph was
the son of Jacob (1:16).

Several solutions have been offered. J. Gresham Machen, in
The Virgin Birth of Christ, analyzed this with customary thor-
oughness suggesting that these are indeed both genealogies of
Joseph but that Matthew gives what Machen calls the "legal"
descendants of David, that is, the line that actually sat upon the
throne (or would have, had it continued) and that Luke gives
the actual paternal line leading to Joseph. He reasons that
Matthew's line does not necessarily indicate literal father-son
relationships but only a list of heirs to the throne, whatever their
relationships to their immediate predecessors may have been.
In this view Heli would be Joseph's literal father. But Jacob (who
presumably had no sons to follow him) would have been Joseph's
immediate predecessor in the "legal" line.[8]

This makes good sense, for Matthew is certainly talking about
heirs to the throne. His is a Jewish Gospel. Moreover, he constructs his genealogy from David onward, asking, Who is the
next heir? By contrast, Luke is interested in actual paternity, so
he constructs his genealogy from Joseph back to David by asking, Who was so-and-so's father?

My only reservation is this: according to Machen's theory
the loose genealogy is Matthew's genealogy. It is not necessarily talking about a literal descent from father to son. Luke's
genealogy on the other hand is about fatherhood and sonship.
But Matthew stresses the descent from father to son by use of

the word "begat"—"Abraham begat Isaac, and Isaac begat Jacob" (the NIV says, "was the father of")—while Luke chooses a looser usage, saying simply "of the" (the NIV translates "son of"). If Luke is talking about strict paternity, he should have used the more precise form.

In my judgment, there is another better solution. This one views the two lines as the lines of Joseph and Mary respectively, each thereby being identified as a descendant of King David. This view was expressed by Bernhard Weiss and Scotland's James Orr. It has received classic expression in a more recent writing by Donald Grey Barnhouse:

> There [are] two genealogies. The lines run parallel from Abraham to David, but then Matthew comes down to Jesus by way of Solomon the son of David, while Luke comes down to Jesus by way of Nathan the son of David. In other words, the two genealogies are the lines of two brothers and the children become cousins. When I state that Luke's genealogy is that of the Virgin Mary and Matthew's genealogy is that of Joseph, I am not merely following the persistent tradition of the early church, as Dr. James Orr states it, but I am setting forth the only explanation that will fit the facts. The whole point of the difference is that Solomon's line was the royal line and Nathan's was the legal line.
>
> For example, the former king of England had an older brother, now the Duke of Windsor, who had a prior claim to the throne of Britain. Suppose that Windsor had been the father of a son by a real queen before he abdicated. It can readily be seen that such a child might be a strong pretender to the throne in case there was no other heir apparent. George VI is in the royal line for he has reigned; any children of Windsor might claim to be in a legal line. Nathan was the older brother of Solomon, but the younger brother took the throne. Nathan's line ran on through the years and ultimately produced the Virgin Mary. Solomon's line ran on through the years and ultimately produced Joseph. Matthew does not say that Joseph begat Jesus, but that he was the husband of Mary, of whom was born Jesus (Matt.

1:16). And Luke uses a word for son that includes what we should call a son-in-law.

But the greatest proof of all lies in one of the names in the account of Matthew: the name Jechonias. It is that name that furnishes the reason for the inclusion of the genealogy of Jesus' step-father, for it proves that Joseph could not have been the father of Jesus, or if he had been, that Jesus could not have been the Messiah. In the use of that name is conclusive evidence that Jesus is the son of Mary and not the son of Joseph. Jechonias was accursed of God with a curse that took the throne away from any of his descendants. "Thus saith the Lord," we read in Jeremiah 22:30, "write ye this man childless, a man that shall not prosper in his days; for no man of his seed shall prosper, sitting upon the throne of David, and ruling any more in Judah" (KJV). Not one of the seven sons of this man could have been king because of the curse of God. If Jesus had been the son of Joseph, he would have been accursed and could never have been the Messiah.

On the other hand, the line of Nathan was not the royal line. A son of Heli would have faced the fact that there was a regal line that would have contested any claim that came from the line of Nathan. How was the dilemma solved? It was solved in a manner that is so simple that it is the utter confusion of the agnostics who seek to tear the Bible to pieces. The answer is this: The line that had no curse upon it produced Heli and his daughter the Virgin Mary and her Son Jesus Christ. He is therefore eligible by the line of Nathan and exhausts that line. The line that had a curse on it produced Joseph and exhausts the line of Solomon, for Joseph's other children now have an elder brother who, legally, by adoption, is the royal heir. How can the title be free in any case? A curse on one line and the lack of reigning royalty in the other.

But when God the Holy Spirit begat the Lord Jesus in the womb of the Virgin without any use of a human father, the child that was born was the seed of David according to the flesh. And when Joseph married Mary and took the unborn child under his protecting care, giving him the title that had come down to him through his ancestor Solomon, the Lord Jesus became the legal Messiah, the royal Messiah, the uncursed Messiah, the true Messiah, the only possible Messiah. The lines are exhausted. Any man that ever comes into this world professing to fulfill the conditions will be a liar and the child of the Devil.[9]

All Scripture Profitable

The obvious conclusion is the value of all Scripture. Second Timothy 3:16 says, "All Scripture is . . . useful." That includes even the genealogies! Even problem genealogies have been used to bring people to faith in Christ.

Ron Blankley, a former area director for Campus Crusade for Christ, was walking through the Student Union of the University of Pennsylvania one day when he saw a student reading a Bible. He remembered Philip's approach to the Ethiopian, so he walked over to him and said, "Do you understand what you're reading?" The student replied, "No, as a matter of fact, I don't. I'm reading the genealogies of Jesus in Matthew and Luke, and I don't understand them because they seem to be different." Blankley had been at Tenth Presbyterian Church the Sunday immediately before this when, curiously enough, I had explained the genealogies exactly as I have just done here. Blankley explained them to this student, and as a result of that explanation the young man came to faith in Jesus Christ as his Savior.

The world has no use for Christ, so it is not surprising that it has no use for Christ's words. But we who know the power of Christ know the power of the Word as well. We should not be afraid to proclaim it, allowing the Spirit of Christ to work even through the alleged problems to bring many to the Savior.

6

THE MOST USEFUL THING
IN THE WORLD

Second Timothy 3:16 reads: "All Scripture is God-breathed and is useful for teaching, rebuking, correcting and training in righteousness." This text is especially suited for Americans since we are so pragmatic and concerned about usefulness. Benjamin Franklin once said of us, "Here we do not ask who a man is or where he comes from; we ask, What can he do?" This text speaks to this and tells us what Scripture can do and why a high view of it is important.

In the early days of the International Council on Biblical Inerrancy, I had the task of finding someone to write a preface for a booklet on "Freedom and Authority" by J. I. Packer. Immediately I thought of Charles Colson, who had served in government under Richard Nixon and had spent time in prison in connection with the prosecutions arising out of the Watergate break-in. He became a Christian just before his imprisonment, and he now spends his time working with prisoners through an organization known as Prison Fellowship. I thought he could talk about the link between freedom and authority with eloquence.

Mr. Colson graciously agreed to write the preface. What I got back was not what I had expected—it was better. He told how, when he had first heard of ICBI, he thought its chief cause—namely, inerrancy—did not concern him. He changed his mind when he saw the effects of the high and low views of Scripture on the front lines of spiritual warfare in the prisons.

> Experiences in the past two years have profoundly altered my thinking. The authority and truth of Scripture is not an obscure issue reserved for the private debate and entertainment of theologians; it is relevant, indeed critical for every serious Christian—layman, pastor, and theologian alike.
>
> My convictions have come, not from studies in Ivory Tower academia, but from life in what may be termed the front-line trenches, behind prison walls where Christians grapple in hand-to-hand combat with the prince of darkness. In our prison fellowships, where the Bible is proclaimed as God's holy and inerrant revelation, believers grow and discipleship deepens. Christians live their faith with power. Where the Bible is not so proclaimed (or where Christianity is presumed to rest on subjective experience alone or contentless fellowship) faith withers and dies. Christianity without biblical fidelity is merely another passing fad in an age of passing fads. In my opinion, the issue is that clear-cut.[1]

I was delighted to have a man of Colson's experience agree with my perception that the issue is this clear-cut.

God-Breathed Scripture

The first thing 2 Timothy 3:16 tells us about Scripture is why it is so useful—because Scripture comes from God.

Old translations of the verse use the word "inspired," reading, "All Scripture is inspired by God." The Latin Vulgate had translated the Greek as *divinitus inspirata,* and *inspirata* passed into English as "inspired" through the translation of Wycliffe. Wycliffe wrote, "Al Scripture of God ynspyred is." The interesting thing about the Greek word is that, strictly speaking, it does not refer to inspiration at all. This is not to say that inspiration is not a valid theological term. It is. When we speak of inspiration we think of the power of God guiding the writers of the Bible so that what they wrote, even though they wrote it in their own language and with their own vocabulary and on the basis of their own experience, was nevertheless exactly what God wanted written. The word *inspiration* refers to this. *Inspiration* means "breathed into," from *in* meaning "in" or "into" and *spiro* meaning "breathe." It describes the process of God's revelation of himself in Scripture from a human point of view. However, this is not the meaning behind the underlying Greek word in 2 Timothy 3:16.

Theopneustos, the Greek word, combines the word for "God" (*theos*) and the word for "breath" or "spirit" (*pneustos*). It means "God-breathed," and is the translation used by the New International Version. It teaches that Scripture is the result of the breathing out of God. Much as God created man by breathing into him and making him a "living soul," God also breathed out the Scriptures so they became a living revelation. Paul is not talking about how human authors of Scripture received God's revelation. He is talking about Scripture itself, saying that the words of Scripture are the words of God, and this is what makes Scripture so useful.

A book containing merely human words might be true and useful to a point. An instruction manual for your new dishwasher helps you run the appliance. The operator's booklet on your new car is useful. If you want to learn Latin, a book teaching you Latin will be useful. But there is no comparison between human books, useful in limited ways, and the Word of God, useful in the ways Paul spells out in his reminder of 2 Timothy 3:16–17.

Perilous Times

In the earlier part of the chapter Paul spoke about perilous days that would come upon the human race. There would come a time when people would love themselves and money, be boastful, proud, abusive, disobedient to parents, ungrateful, unholy, without love. If there were ever verses describing our age, they are these, although they also describe every pagan age in history. The tragedy of these verses is that they also speak about the specific context in which these horrors can be found, and it is not the culture at large. It is the visible church. Paul said these vices will be found among those who have a "form of godliness" but deny its power. These are not out-and-out pagans, those who have nothing to do with religion; they are those professing Christians who do not know its power or reality.

But if this is coming, and if this is the kind of thing Paul was warning young Timothy against, isn't Paul going to give Timothy something special to help him through these troublesome times? We wait breathlessly. We say, Paul, what are you going to offer Timothy to help him resist a horror like the one you are describing—when the culture and values of the world actually permeate the church?

We wait for a new revelation. What Paul gives is quite different. He says, Timothy, I am not going to give you anything new. All I want you to do is continue as you have, continue in what you have learned, because you know those from whom you learned it—because you hold in your hand the very words of God. These are useful for dealing with any problem you will face in the church or out of the church, at this time or at any other period of history.

When Paul admonishes Timothy to continue in what he has learned because he *knows those from whom he learned it,* Paul was probably looking ahead to what he was about to say concerning Scripture, that it is God-breathed. Although the intermediate source of Timothy's spiritual knowledge may have been his mother or grandmother, or even Paul himself, the ultimate source was the self-revealing God. And this is what gives the teaching usefulness. What Timothy learned was not of human devising; it was not human ideas or theories. It was what God had revealed in Scripture, and Paul wanted Timothy to continue in that because of its source.

Uses of Scripture

Paul next talked about the categories of usefulness. There are four. Scripture is "useful for teaching, rebuking, correcting and training in righteousness."

Teaching

Because Christianity is in many ways preeminently a teaching religion, Paul started with teaching. Apart from the truth of God, we flounder in spiritual and mental darkness. It is only the Word of God that brings light. Where the gospel has gone the light of God has burst through human darkness. In our churches, Sunday by Sunday, and in other meetings throughout the week, we teach the Word of God. We do not merely motivate. We do not have group-therapy sessions. We do not merely celebrate our common convictions. We teach God's Word. In the pages of his book God has disclosed certain truths about himself and his creation, including ourselves, and we need to know these things. In a certain sense, all growth that comes into our Christian lives has its origin in the things we are taught from Scripture as the Holy Spirit takes these and applies them to our lives.

Left to ourselves we get everything backward. First Corinthians 2:14 says, "The man without the Spirit does not accept the things that come from the Spirit of God, for they are foolishness to him, and he cannot understand them, because they are spiritually discerned." In other words, the truth of God appears foolish to the natural man. We hear about the character of God, and we think God can't be like that. It just doesn't make sense. Only a fool would believe that. Or we hear what God says about our own nature and say That can't be right. I don't think that's true of me. Only a fool would believe that. We count God's truth as foolishness and in counting it foolish, we actually prove ourselves to be fools.

Even when talking about the true character of God, there is nothing we can say that is not contrary to the thinking of the natural human mind. We might agree on certain words. We might say God is love, and the unsaved person might say yes, all right, God is love. But he does not mean the same thing we mean when we use the word. The unsaved person has his own idea of what love means, an indulgent, sentimental love. But we mean a demanding, holy, jealous, purifying love, and this is quite different.

Sovereignty is the most important attribute of God, and sovereignty bothers the unsaved immensely. In a certain sense, people recognize that if there is a God, he must be sovereign because a God who does not rule his own universe is no God at all. If he does not rule, something or someone else rules, and that other thing is the true God. God must rule. But the natural man does not like that, so he resists God's sovereignty. That is one reason it is so difficult to preach the gospel. Deep in his heart the unsaved individual knows that if God is God, he is at least sovereign, and such a man hates God for his sovereignty.

That is why Adam rebelled against God. God put the tree of the knowledge of good and evil in the Garden of Eden and said, "You shall not eat of this tree, because the day in which you eat of it you will die." Adam was offended by this. He was not fooled by Satan's arguments, as Eve was (1 Tim. 2:14). He disobeyed in full knowledge of what he was doing. In essence Adam shook his fist in God's face, saying, God, I hate the restriction you have placed upon me, because it means you are sovereign and I am not, and I want to be sovereign in my own life. I want to rule things myself; I want to do things my way. So, if you say, "Don't eat of that tree," that is the one thing I want to do. And I am going to eat of it and die—whatever that may be. Adam did eat of it, and that same spirit of rebellion (and death) passed onto the human race.

When Jesus Christ came, his contemporaries said the same thing: We will not have this man rule over us. So they crucified him! Crucifixion is the response of the unsaved human heart to God's sovereignty: I want to do things the way I want to do them, and I will not acknowledge God's right to interfere. Yet, sovereignty is one of the first things we are taught in Scripture concerning God's character. He is the sovereign God, and he is sovereign whether we acknowledge it or not.

We must also be taught about God's holiness and omniscience because we do not like these either. If God is holy, it means we are not holy. If God is the standard for measuring our morality, our morality looks very dirty. Since nobody wants to look morally dirty, we hate God for his holiness. We hate God for his omniscience, too. Omniscience means God knows everything, but we do not want to be known. We want people to know us a little, but we resist letting ourselves be known in a deep way.

Some time ago I read a book on body language by Julius Fast. Fast discusses nonverbal communication. For example, someone comes to your home to visit you at 10:30 P.M., when you are just thinking about getting into bed. He says, "Hi! Here I am! Just thought I'd stop in for a little bit." As you barely suppress a yawn, you say, "It's good to see you; come on in." But as you say this, you fold your arms like a barrier. With this body language, you are not truly saying it's good to see him; your folded arms mean you wish your guest would go away and come back another time.

One section in Fast's *Body Language* talks about staring. It is quite all right to stare at an object, Fast maintains. If someone goes into a museum and sees a painting he likes, he can go over to it, fix his attention on it, and stare at it for a long time. He can look at the object for fifteen minutes, twenty minutes, thirty minutes. Nobody minds at all. People will even compliment him as a lover of great art! But now, Fast writes, suppose that instead of staring at an object he decides to stare at a person. Suppose the next time somebody comes into the room you try this out. Look right at him and don't take your eyes off him. He will soon turn away and then look back to find you are still staring. He will look away again. If you are still staring, he will say, "Why are you staring at me? What's wrong? Am I not dressed properly? Do I have a spot on my shirt? Isn't my hair combed? What's wrong?"

We become very uneasy when someone stares at us because we associate staring with prying. Someone is trying to get to know us too well, trying to figure out what we are like, what we are thinking. Because we are ashamed of what we really are— we do not admit that openly, but that is the truth—we turn away, saying, Stop staring at me; I don't like that. If you don't stop, I'm going to punch you in the nose. If that is the way we function on the merely human level, with other people who cannot actually see within, what is our reaction to Almighty God who sees everything, before whom all hearts are open, all desires known?

Jonathan Edwards once preached a sermon called, "Men Naturally Are God's Enemies."[2] In his very thorough fashion, Edwards examined those characteristics of God abhorrent to the natural man. He wrote that people hate God for his sovereignty because they want to be sovereign themselves. They hate God for his holiness because they are not holy and God's holiness is an offense to them. They hate God for his omniscience because they do not want to be known intimately. But there is one more thing people hate God for, Edwards said, and that is his immutability. Immutability means God does not change; he is always the same. Why should this be offensive to the natural man? Because God's immutability means he does not change in any of his attributes, and the natural man hates them all.

One of the great uses of Scripture is to teach us—in spite of ourselves, our instincts, our likes, and dislikes—what God is really like. God is not something we can mold into our own image. We cannot make him acceptable to our way of thinking. God is who God is. The beginning of wisdom is knowledge of the Holy One and "the knowledge of the Holy One is understanding," as it says in Proverbs 9:10.

When looking at the Bible's usefulness for teaching, we are not merely talking about what the Bible teaches about God but also what the Bible teaches us about ourselves. The Bible teaches us that we are not like God. As a matter of fact, it teaches that we are in rebellion against God yet that we need him. It is only when we begin to explore the Bible that we discover ourselves and are turned back from sin to God, in whom our true help is found.

A former professor at Princeton Theological Seminary, Dr. Emile Cailliet, wrote a book entitled *Journey into Light,* the story of his conversion. He had been brought up with a naturalistic education and had never seen a Bible. World War I came. As he sat in the trenches he found himself reflecting on the inadequacy of his world-and-life view. He asked himself where life came from and what it all meant? What value were theories in the face of reality?

During the long night watches, Cailliet began to long for what he came to call "a book that would understand me." Although highly educated, he knew of no such book. Later, after being released from the army and returning to his studies, he determined to prepare one secretly for his personal use. As he read for his courses, he filed away passages that spoke to his condition. Afterward he copied them in a leather-bound book, hoping the quotations, carefully indexed and numbered, would lead him from fear and anguish to release and jubilation.

At last the day came when he had put the finishing touches to his book. Cailliet sat down under a tree and opened the anthology. He began to read, but instead of release and jubilation, a growing disappointment came over him as he recognized that, instead of speaking to his condition, the passages only reminded him of their context and of his own work in searching them out. He realized the whole project would not work. The book was of his own making. It carried no strength of persuasion. Dejected, he returned it to his pocket.

At that very moment his wife (who, incidentally, knew nothing of the project) came by and related an interesting story. She had been walking in their tiny French village and had stumbled upon a Huguenot chapel. Having never seen it before, she surprised herself when she went in and asked for a Bible. The elderly pastor had given her one. Cailliet's wife apologized to her husband, for she knew his feelings about the Christian faith.

He was not listening to her apology. "A Bible, you say? Where is it? Show me," he said. When she produced it he rushed to his study and devoured its pages.

Here is his description of what happened:

> I opened it and "chanced" upon the Beatitudes! I read, and read, and read—now aloud with an indescribable warmth surging within. . . . I could not find words to express my awe and wonder. And suddenly the realization dawned upon me: This was the Book that would understand me! I continued to read deeply into the night, mostly from the gospels. And lo and behold, as I looked through them, the One of whom they spoke, the One who spoke and acted in them, became alive to me. . . . The providential circumstances amid which the Book had found me now made it clear that while it seemed absurd to speak of a book understanding a man, this could be said of the Bible because its pages were animated by the presence of the living God and the power of his mighty acts. To this God I prayed that night, and the God who answered was the same God of whom it was spoken in the Book.[3]

The Bible is useful for teaching in many other ways, too. It also teaches us about Jesus Christ, who is the solution to our problems. Indeed, the Bible points to Jesus, and this is accomplished when the Holy Spirit moves us to faith in him and his redemptive work. This is what Jesus meant when he said, "When the Counselor comes, whom I will send to you from the Father, the Spirit of truth who goes out from the Father, he will testify about me" (John 15:26). Since the role of the Holy Spirit is to point to Jesus in the Scriptures, we can be sure we are listening to the voice of the Holy Spirit when that happens.

But isn't the Bible mostly history? a person might ask. The Old Testament doesn't talk about Jesus. How can the Spirit point us to him? The answer is that Jesus becomes the subject of the Old Testament by fitting into its general themes and by fulfilling the specific prophecies found there.

One main Old Testament theme is sin and the resulting need of man. The Bible begins with the story of creation. No sooner is this story told (in the first and second chapters of Genesis) than we are told of the fall of Adam and Eve. Instead of being humbly and gratefully dependent upon his Creator, as he should have been, Adam was soon in a state of rebellion against God. In going his own way, the consequences of sin and ultimately death passed onto the race.

In the rest of the Old Testament, these consequences unfold: the murder of Abel, the corruption leading to the flood, demonism, sexual perversions, and eventually tragedy for the chosen nation of Israel in spite of great blessings. David summarizes the Old Testament in his great psalm of repentance, a psalm for the whole human race:

> Have mercy on me, O God,
>   according to your unfailing love;
> according to your great compassion
>   blot out my transgressions.
> Wash away all my iniquity,
>   and cleanse me from my sin.
> For I know my transgressions,
>   and my sin is always before me. . . .

Surely I have been a sinner from birth,
　　sinful from the time my mother conceived me.
                                                    Psalm 51:1–3, 5

The truth of man's sin is expounded in the Bible because the Bible is also able to point to Christ as the solution to man's dilemma.

A second great Old Testament theme is God's love for sinners. When Adam and Eve sinned, sin separated them from the Creator. They tried to hide. But God came to them in the cool of the evening, calling. God spoke in judgment, as he had to do, and he revealed the consequences of their sin. Still, he also killed animals, clothed the man and woman with skins, covered their shame, and began his teaching of the way of salvation through sacrifice. In the same story he spoke to Satan, revealing the coming of One who would defeat him forever: "He will crush your head, and you will strike his heel" (Gen. 3:15).

Nine chapters later we find another, somewhat veiled reference to the "seed" who will crush Satan. God's first great promise to Abraham stresses that in him all nations would be blessed (Gen. 12:3; cf. 22:18). This blessing certainly would not come through Abraham personally. It would not come through all Jews indiscriminately, for all Jews are not even theists. The blessing foretold was to come through the seed of Abraham, the promised seed, the Messiah. Years later the apostle Paul used this text to show that the seed was the Lord Jesus, the promise to Abraham was one of blessing through him, and the blessing was to come through Christ's great work of redemption (Gal. 3:13–16).

In the Book of Numbers the Lord speaks an interesting prophecy through Balaam, that shifty, pagan prophet of Moses' day. Balak, a king who was hostile to Israel, hired Balaam to curse the Jewish people. However, every time Balaam opened his mouth to curse the Jews, blessings came out. On one occasion Balaam said, "A star will come out of Jacob; a scepter will rise out of Israel. . . . A ruler will come out of Jacob" (Num. 24:17, 19).

In the same way the patriarch Jacob, as he lay dying, spoke about Jesus when he prophesied, "The scepter will not depart from Judah, nor the ruler's staff from between his feet, until he comes to whom it belongs; and the obedience of the nations is his" (Gen. 49:10). Moses also foretold the one who would come: "The Lord your God will raise up for you a prophet like me from among your own brothers. You must listen to him" (Deut. 18:15). Later in that same passage God spoke to Moses: "I will put my words in his mouth, and he will tell them everything I command him" (v. 18).

The psalms contain great prophecies. Psalm 2 tells of Christ's rule over the nations of this earth. Psalm 16 foretells the resurrection (v. 10; cf. Acts 2:31). In Psalms 22, 23, and 24 we have three portraits of the Lord Jesus: the suffering Savior, the compassionate Shepherd, and the King. Other psalms speak of other aspects of his life and person. Psalm 110 returns to the theme of his rule, looking to the day when Jesus shall take his seat at the right hand of the Father and all his enemies shall be made his footstool.

Details of Christ's life, death, and resurrection occur in the books of the prophets—in Isaiah, Daniel, Jeremiah, Ezekiel, Hosea, Zechariah, and others. The Lord Jesus Christ and his work are the chief subjects of the Bible. It is the work of the Holy Spirit to reveal him. As this takes place the Bible becomes understandable, Scripture bears witness to Scripture, and the authority and power of the living God surge through its pages.

Rebuking and Correcting

The Word of God is also useful for rebuking and correcting (2 Tim. 3:16). Rebuking means calling our attention to wrong things in our lives. Correcting means setting those wrong things right.

Some years ago I knew a French woman who had a young son. On one occasion she said to him, "Jean Claude, I'm going to the store, but I have just made some strawberry jam. I know you like strawberry jam, but I don't want you to get into it, so I'm putting it on this high shelf. Don't touch it until I come back."

After his mother left the room, the son looked longingly at the strawberry jam trying to figure a way to get into it. He moved a chair from the table in the middle of the kitchen and pushed it over to the counter. Then he stepped from the floor onto the chair and from the chair onto the counter. As he stood on the counter, the boy reached his arm up to get the jar only to discover the jar was so big he could not get his hand around it. But his reach was high enough to stick his finger over the edge and down into the jam. He poked his finger into the jam, then pulled it out and licked it. Suddenly he heard his mother. Quickly he scurried down from the counter to the chair and from the chair to the floor. Then he placed the chair back by the table in the middle of the kitchen.

His mother walked through the door and said, "Jean Claude, have you been into the strawberry jam?"

Deciding this was a good time to lie, the boy replied, "No, Mother, I haven't been into the jam." He looked her right in the eye as he said it.

His mother was not convinced. She asked again, "Jean Claude, have you been in the jam?"

This time he could not quite look her in the eye. He dropped his eyes a bit but kept the same story. "No, Mother," he responded, "I haven't been in the jam."

She questioned him a third time. His eyes fell a little farther now. He stared at her shoes. Still he maintained, "No, Mother, I haven't been in the jam."

She asked him a fourth time, "Jean Claude, have you been in the jam?" This time his eyes fell so low he realized why she kept asking him the question. Right there in the middle of his white shirt was a big red spot of strawberry jam!

This is the way the Bible works on us as God brings reproof and correction. We read a verse such as John 13:35: "All men will know that you are my disciples if you love one another."

Immediately we apply it—to somebody else. We say, Joe Smith should certainly read that because he acts in a very unloving way. The Holy Spirit nudges us to read it again, and as we do we think, Well, you know, it's not only Joe Smith who needs to read it; everybody does. The third time we read the passage we reply, Yes, even somebody like me. After the fourth time, we begin to understand why the Holy Spirit is bringing this verse to our attention. We remember what it is we said to offend Joe Smith and make him react badly to us. At this point we are ready to confess the sin and correct it.

The written works of men and women flatter us because the writers are sinners like ourselves who also want to escape the searing gaze of God. We do not receive the reproof we need from the works of mere men and women. We receive it from God, as little by little he exposes our sin and leads us into the path of righteousness.

Training in Righteousness

Paul's last direction is that the Bible is useful for training, training in righteousness. This is not the same thing as teaching, mentioned earlier. The word used here involves the kind of consistent and habitual training a tutor does with a child. Paul's point was that we are children in the faith and we have to learn over a period of years just like children have to learn throughout childhood. God's way is often not to teach us one big lesson at one time, but to teach us little by little. As it says in Isaiah, "It is: Do and do, do and do, rule on rule, rule on rule, a little here, a little there" (Isa. 28:10). Inch by inch God directs our attention to Christ's teaching and makes us increasingly strong and settled. Only if we study Scripture on a regular basis and grow in daily fellowship with the Lord will this happen.

A friend of mine who is a great baritone singer gave me an illustration for Psalm 32:8. This passage reads, "I will lead you in the way that you should go. I will guide you with mine eye" (KJV). My friend described how in the early days of his marriage he found a slight flaw in his wife, a marvelous Christian woman. He had a wonderful baritone voice, but his wife's voice sometimes got a bit squeaky—especially when she got excited in conversation. At such times it would rise higher and higher. My friend thought, I have to deal with this, or I'm going to end up hating the sound of my wife's voice. He devised this plan.

One day when he was in the kitchen helping his wife with the dishes, my friend said, "Dear, do you know what they teach an actress when she first begins to learn acting?"

"No," she replied.

"They teach her to lower her voice."

"Oh."

"Yes," he continued. "You know, a woman's voice is naturally high, and they usually teach her to lower it about an octave. Whatever she says, she is to count down eight notes and then say it again. I think your voice would be helped if you would do that. But, you know, I think we need a signal in order for you to know when your voice is getting higher."

So, they worked out a sign. My friend would tuck in his chin when his wife needed to lower her voice.

This produced some funny situations. They would be sitting around the dining room table with guests and the conversation would get animated. His wife's voice would begin to rise. My friend would tuck in his chin. Sometimes while still talking, his wife would glance down the table, see his tucked-in chin, and suddenly drop her voice a full octave!

We need to get into a similar habit spiritually. God knows our voices are sometimes shrill. He knows we will often act in unbecoming and displeasing ways. He knows we will sin. But he wants us to get into the habit of looking to him on a regular basis through our daily study of Scripture. If we do, he will catch our eye and lead us in the way we should go.

God's desire is for every man and woman of God to develop the character of the Lord Jesus. This does not happen automatically. It does not happen by wishful thinking. The world and its values will not accomplish it. It will only happen as we are taught, rebuked, corrected, and trained by Scripture, thus becoming "thoroughly equipped for every good work" (2 Tim. 3:17).

We live in an evil, rebellious, self-centered, and vacillating world. How is a Christian to stand and even to prosper in such times? There is only one way, by standing upon the firm foundation God himself has provided for us:

> How firm a foundation, ye saints of the Lord,
> Is laid for your faith in his excellent Word!

I trust you will take your stand on this foundation, perhaps as a result of this book, perhaps through the encouragement of a fellow believer. Best of all, I trust you will do so through your own study of the Bible. There is no more useful activity or necessary task than filling your heart and mind with the treasures of God's authoritative and inerrant revelation.

7

THE SUFFICIENCY OF SCRIPTURE

I have been senior pastor at Tenth Presbyterian Church for twenty-five years. One of the blessings of serving there is that for over the one hundred and sixty-five years of its distinguished history (1829–1994) the church has stood for the priority of the Bible as the Word of God. That priority has been both doctrinal and practical—doctrinal because the elders and most of the people believe the Bible to be the Word of God, the only infallible rule of faith and practice, and practical because the leaders also believe the Bible is a treasure to be constantly valued and followed in the church's life. This was true from the days of

Thomas A. McAuley, the first pastor (1829–1833), and Henry Augustus Boardman, the first minister to serve a long pastorate (1833–1876). It is best illustrated by an incident from the early days of the ministry of Donald Grey Barnhouse (1927–1960), who had a profound and personal influence on my own idea of what the ministry should be.

A week or two after Barnhouse became pastor of Tenth Church, he entered the pulpit one Sunday morning and opened the pulpit Bible to a point near the middle, where he then placed his sermon notes, his Bible, and a hymn book. As he looked down at the Bible pages he noticed that the words were part of a curse upon those nations that do not know God. It occurred to him that he would like to have before him a passage containing words of some great promise about Scripture.

He opened the Bible to Isaiah 55:10–11:

> As the rain and the snow
>   come down from heaven,
> and do not return to it
>   without watering the earth
> and making it bud and flourish,
>   so that it yields seed for the sower and bread
>   for the eater,
> So is my word that goes out from my mouth:
>   It will not return to me empty,
> but will accomplish what I desire
>   and achieve the purpose for which I sent it.

To his surprise Barnhouse discovered that his predecessors had apparently done the same thing for decades. The edges of the Bible were worn in half circles curving inward from the bindings at this text, and the pages were torn and mended. As he later observed, those pages "containing the great fifty-fifth chapter of Isaiah and the preceding page with the fifty-third chapter of Isaiah concerning the Lord Jesus Christ as God's Lamb, give mute evidence that the men who have stood in the pulpit of

Tenth Church for more than a century were men of the living Word and the written Word."[1]

Later Barnhouse discovered another section of the Bible that was similarly worn. It was the great psalm of the Bible, Psalm 119. Evidently, his predecessors, finding it difficult to keep their notes on the Isaiah pages, searched for another passage to remind them of the power and priority of God's Word. Barnhouse told this story in a memorial booklet marking the twenty-fifth anniversary of his pastorate. He concluded this way:

> It is my prayer that no man shall ever stand in this pulpit as long as time shall last who does not desire to have all that he does based upon this Book. For this Book does not *contain* the Word of God, it is the Word of God. And though we may preach the Word with all the stammering limitations of our human nature, the grace of God does the miracle of the ministry, and through human lips speaks the divine Word, and the hearts of the people are refreshed. There is no other explanation for the continuing power of a church that is poorly located, that is without endowment, but which continues to draw men and women to the capacity of its seating arrangements, morning and evening, summer and winter, and which sends its sons and daughters by the score to preach the unsearchable riches of Christ throughout the world.[2]

Inerrancy and Sufficiency

About ten years into my own pastorate, at the end of 1977 and the beginning of 1978, I became chairman of the International Council on Biblical Inerrancy. The need for this Council stemmed from the fact that in the 1970s the evangelical church was drifting from its roots. Professors in prominent evangelical institutions were teaching that the Bible contained errors of historical and scientific fact but that this didn't matter. We believed that it did matter and tackled this deviation head on.

We held three gatherings of prominent evangelical scholars to hammer out three documents of "affirmation and denial," which became nearly creedal in some quarters. The first was on inerrancy itself (The Chicago Statement on Biblical Inerrancy), the second on sound principles of interpretation (The Chicago Statement on Biblical Hermeneutics), and the third on the application of the Bible to contemporary issues (The Chicago Statement on Biblical Application). These documents are printed as appendices to this volume.

We also held two large lay conferences, the first in San Diego in the spring of 1982 and the second in Washington in the fall of 1988.

Since many believed it should be enough merely to believe the Bible is trustworthy in areas of faith and morals, we were often asked why inerrancy was important. It was not that simple. To begin, the Bible is an historical book and Christianity is an historical religion. If the Bible errs in matters of historical fact, Christianity itself is affected.

One hundred years of German "historical Jesus" research proved that. The scholars involved in that movement wanted to separate the Christ of faith from the Jesus of history, finding out who was the true Jesus. However, as Albert Schweitzer proved in his classic study, *The Quest for the Historical Jesus*, what they succeeded in doing was transforming Jesus into the scholars' own images. Rationalists produced a rationalist Jesus, socialists a socialistic Jesus, moralists a moralistic Jesus, and so on. The attempt to have Christianity without its historical base failed.

If part of the Bible is true and part is not, who is to tell us what the true parts are? There are only two answers to this question. Either we must make the decision ourselves, so the truth becomes subjective, merely what appeals to me. Or else, it is the scholar who tells us what we can believe and what we cannot believe. The Council argued that God had not left us to the whims of scholars. He had given us a reliable book to read and understand ourselves.

I wrestled with the inerrancy of the Bible during my seminary years. It is not that I questioned it. Anyone who had been raised with the teaching of Donald Grey Barnhouse and others like him could hardly doubt that God had given us an inerrant revelation. My problem was that my professors did not believe this, and much of what I heard in the classroom was meant to reveal the book's errors so students would not depend on it too deeply. What was a student to do? The professors seemed to have all the facts. How could a professor be challenged when he argued that recent scholarship had shown that the old simplistic views about inerrancy were no longer valid? Didn't we have to admit that the Bible was filled with errors?

As I worked on this I discovered some interesting things. First, the problems imagined in the Bible were hardly new concerns. For the most part they were known centuries ago, even by such ancient theologians as Saint Augustine and Saint Jerome, who debated apparent contradictions in their correspondence. I also discovered that the results of sound scholarship have not tended to uncover more problems, as my professors were suggesting. Rather they have tended to resolve problems and show that what were once thought to be errors are not errors at all. (I illustrated this in chapter five.)

However, important as the matter of inerrancy is, I do not think it is the most critical biblical issue facing the American church at the present time in this last decade of the twentieth century.

The issue I would pinpoint is the *sufficiency* of God's Word. The questions surrounding this are numerous. Do we really believe God has given us what we need in this book? Or do we think we have to supplement the Bible with other man-made things? Do we need sociological techniques to do evangelism? Must we attract people to our churches by showmanship and entertainment? Do we need psychology and psychiatry for Christian growth? Do we need extra-biblical signs or miracles for guidance? Is the Bible's teaching adequate for achieving social progress and reform?

I believe this is important because it is possible to believe that the Bible is the inerrant Word of God, the only infallible rule of faith and practice (as many if not all evangelicals claim to do) and yet neglect it. In doing this, we effectually repudiate it just because we think it is not really adequate for today's tasks and that other ideas need to be brought in to supplement the revelation. This is exactly what many evangelicals, evangelical churches, and evangelical institutions are doing.

The Bible's Own Testimony

As I have become alert to this problem, I have also noted how the Bible deals directly with it. Psalm 19, Matthew 4, and 2 Timothy 3 are probably the three most important passages in the Bible about the nature of the Word of God. The first contrasts it with God's general revelation. The second shows how Jesus used the Bible to overcome temptation. The third is Paul's advice to Timothy in view of the terrible times he saw coming. But notice: each passage stresses that the Word of God is alone sufficient for these challenges.

Psalm 19 speaks about the wonderful revelation of God in nature. It continues:

> The law of the LORD is *perfect*,
>   reviving the soul.
> The statutes of the LORD are *trustworthy*,
>   making wise the simple.
> The precepts of the LORD are *right*,
>   giving joy to the heart.
> The commands of the LORD are *radiant*,
>   giving light to the eyes.
> The fear of the LORD is *pure*,
>   enduring forever.
> The ordinances of the LORD are *sure*
>   and altogether righteous.

> They are more *precious* than gold,
>   than much pure gold;
> They are *sweeter* than honey,
>   than honey from the comb.
> By them is your servant *warned*,
>   and in keeping them there is great *reward*.
>   Psalm 19:7–11, *emphasis mine*

The revelation of God in nature is wonderful but limited. By contrast, the revelation of God in Scripture is perfect, trustworthy, right, radiant, pure, sure, precious, sweet, and rewarding. By what language would it be possible for the psalmist more effectively to emphasize the complete and utter sufficiency of God's Word?

In Matthew 4 we discover the sufficiency of the Word of God in times of temptation. Through quotations from Deuteronomy 8:3, 6:13, and 6:16 Jesus withstood Satan. Jesus did not reason with Satan without Scripture. He did not resort to supernatural power or ask God for some special sign or intervention. He knew the Bible, stood on it, and used it forcefully.

Second Timothy 3:1–5 is the same. As I pointed out in chapter 6, Paul warns his young protege against the terrible times he sees coming. They will be times like ours, days in which "people will be lovers of themselves, lovers of money, boastful, proud, abusive, disobedient to their parents, ungrateful, unholy, without love, unforgiving, slanderous, without self-control, brutal, not lovers of the good, treacherous, rash, conceited, lovers of pleasure rather than lovers of God." And if that is not terrible enough, they will be days in which these vices will be found even in the churches. For they will be found among those "having a form of godliness but denying its power."

What is Timothy to do when such times come? Surely Paul must have some secret new weapon, some unexpected trick for him to use. No. As we saw earlier, instead of something new, we find Paul recommending what Timothy has had all along—the Word of God—because the Bible is sufficient even for terrible times like these. "But as for you, continue in what you have learned and have become convinced of, because you know those from whom you learned it, and how from infancy you have known the holy Scriptures, which are able to make you wise for salvation through faith in Christ Jesus" (2 Tim. 3:14–15).

But it is not only that the Word of God is sufficient for all times, even times like ours. It is also sufficient in all areas. That is, it is able to do all we need it to do and are commissioned to do as Christians.

Sufficient for Evangelism

The Word of God is sufficient for evangelism. The only way the Holy Spirit works to regenerate lost men and women is through the Word of God. In fact, it is the only thing that really works. Everything else—captivating music, moving testimonies, emotional appeals, even coming forward to make a personal commitment to Jesus Christ is at best supplementary. And if it is used apart from the faithful preaching and teaching of the Word of God, the resulting conversions are spurious, meaning those who respond become Christians in name only.

Peter said, "You have been born again, not of perishable seed, but of imperishable, through the living and enduring word of God" (1 Peter 1:23). The problem is many people do not believe this and want to depend on other things. Some, like Charles Finney, depend on evangelistic techniques. Others, like those in the popular and growing Vineyard Movement, believe the way to do evangelism is by "signs and wonders."

Luke 16:19–31 contains a story that addresses this problem. Jesus described a rich man and a poor beggar named Lazarus. Both died. Lazarus was carried into the presence of Abraham in paradise, and the rich man went to hell. At first the rich man asked Abraham to send Lazarus to comfort him. When that was declared impossible he asked that Lazarus be sent back to earth to warn his brothers of their pending judgment, since they were as wicked as himself. "I beg you, father, send Lazarus to my father's house, for I have five brothers. Let him warn them, so that they will not also come to this place of torment."

Abraham replied, "They have Moses and the Prophets; let them listen to them."

The rich man persisted, "No, father Abraham, but if someone from the dead goes to them, they will repent."

Abraham's final word and the climactic point of the parable was: "If they do not listen to Moses and the Prophets, they will not be convinced even if someone rises from the dead" (vv. 27–31).

Paul also says this in Romans 10:6–9. It is exactly what Moses was saying in the verses from Deuteronomy 30 quoted by Paul:

> The righteousness that is by faith says: "Do not say in your heart, 'Who will ascend into heaven?'" (that is, to bring Christ down) "or 'Who will descend into the deep?'" (that is, to bring Christ up from the dead). But what does it say? "The word is near you; it is in your mouth and in your heart," that is, the word of faith we are proclaiming: That if you confess with your mouth, "Jesus is Lord," and believe in your heart that God raised him from the dead, you will be saved.

The people had been given Moses and the prophets. According to Moses, the word was "near" them, in their mouths and hearts (Deut. 30:14). That was sufficient. If they did not heed the written word, repent of their sin, and turn to God in faith on the basis of that given revelation, they would not be changed even by a religion of miracles. No number of "signs and wonders," however great, would save them.

People have the Christian gospel today, says Paul, in exactly the same way and this is "the word of faith we are proclaiming." That gospel is here, and because it is being proclaimed, all possible excuses for failing to believe in Christ and be saved from the coming judgment are eliminated.

During my decade as Chairman of the International Council on Biblical Inerrancy (1978–1988), I listened to many sermons on the Bible and preached quite a few myself. Dr. W. A. Criswell, pastor of the First Baptist Church of Dallas, gave the best I heard at ICBI's first "Summit Meeting" in Chicago in the fall of 1978.

At the time Criswell had been pastor of the First Baptist Church of Dallas for over thirty-five years and had been in the ministry for more than fifty years. He had been chosen to address this amazing gathering of 350 pastors, scholars, and leaders of the major para-church organizations on the subject "What Happens When I Preach the Bible as Literally True?" His answer was a tour de force, as he explained what had happened to himself, what had happened to his church, and what he believes happens to God when God's Word is used and honored.

About a year after he became pastor of the Dallas church, he announced to his well-established congregation that he was going to preach through the Bible, beginning with Genesis and going right on to the last benedictory prayer in Revelation. "You never heard such lugubrious prognostications," he reported. People said it would kill the church. Nobody would come to hear someone preach about Habakkuk, Haggai, and Nahum. Most people didn't even know who those biblical books or characters were, they said. Criswell did it all the same, and to everyone's astonishment the problem that developed was not at all what they expected. They did not have to deal with the demise of the church but rather had to decide where to put all the people who were pressing in weekly to hear such biblical preaching. There were thousands of conversions, and today the First Baptist Church of Dallas is one of the largest, most effective and biblically sound churches in the entire country.[3]

Scoffers abound. Critics multiply. But the lesson of history is the unique power of the Bible to regenerate lost sinners, transform their lives, and build churches.

Sufficient for Sanctification

I have been preaching on the Book of Romans for the past seven years and have discovered many interesting things in that time. The most significant has been Paul's approach to sanctification, an approach not at all what we would expect or what many people would desire. When we think of sanctification today, most of us think about one of two things. We think about a method (Here are three steps to sanctification; do this and you will be holy), or else we think of an experience (You need a second work of grace, a baptism of the Holy Spirit, or something). Paul's approach is to know the Bible and its teaching on God's plan for salvation.

Paul makes this clear in the sixth chapter where he says, "In the same way, count yourselves dead to sin but alive to God in Christ Jesus" (v. 11). This is the first time Paul tells his readers to do something. What they must do is "count" or "reckon upon" the fact that God has done an irreversible work in their lives, and as a result they have died to sin (the Greek verb is in the past tense, it is an aorist) and have been made alive to God in Christ Jesus.

The only way they can understand what has happened to them is to know the Bible because this teaches them what has happened. But then they are to go on with God, acting on the basis of what has been done. In other words, they cannot go back to being what they were before. They are new creatures in Christ. The only thing they can do is get on with living the Christian life. They must go forward.

The Bible's approach to sanctification has nothing to do with either a method or an experience. It has everything to do with knowing and living by the sufficient Word of God.

Sufficient for Guidance

In 1993 it was my privilege to introduce the Reverend Phillip D. Jensen, the minister of St. Matthias Church in Sydney, Australia, to America through the spring meetings of the Philadelphia Conference on Reformed Theology. It was his first time in the United States.

Among other works, Phillip Jensen wrote a book entitled *The Last Word on Guidance*. The sole point of this work was that the "last word on guidance" is the Bible. It is what God has given us to indicate how we are to live and what we are to do to please him. Everything we need is in the Bible. If there is something we want or think we need that is not in the Bible—what job we should take, whom we should marry, where we should live—it doesn't matter as long as we obey God's teachings about living a godly life.

Does God not have a plan for our lives in these areas? He does. He has a detailed plan for all things, having preordained "whatsoever comes to pass," as the Westminster Confession of Faith has it. But we do not have to know this plan in advance and, indeed, we cannot know it. What we can know and need to know is what God has told us in the Bible.

What has he told us? In the eighth chapter of Romans he provides a general pattern for what he is doing with us. This includes being delivered from God's judgment upon us for our sin and from sin's power and being made increasingly like Jesus Christ. The five decisive steps of this plan are: (1) foreknowledge, (2) predestination, (3) effectual calling, (4) justification, and (5) glorification (vv. 29–30).

There are also many specific matters. The Ten Commandments contain some of these. It is God's will that we have no other gods before him, that we do not worship even him by the use of images, that we do not misuse his name, that we remember the Sabbath by keeping it holy, that we honor our parents, that we do not murder or commit adultery or steal or give false testimony or covet (cf. Exod. 20). The Lord Jesus Christ amplified many of these commandments and added others, above all teaching that we are to "love each other" (John 15:12).

It is God's will that we be holy (1 Thess. 4:3). It is God's will that we should pray (1 Thess. 5:17). In the twelfth chapter of

Romans Paul says, "Do not conform any longer to the pattern of this world, but be transformed by the renewing of your mind. Then you will be able to test and approve what God's will is— his good, pleasing and perfect will" (v. 2).

If we seek guidance—and we should—texts like these will give it to us. As to the other, lesser matters that fill so much of our thinking—What job shall I take? Where shall I live? Whom shall I marry?—in such areas, after having prayed for God's providential guidance, we are free to do whatever seems best to us, knowing that the God who cares for us will always keep us in his way. This is sound theology.

Sufficient for Social Reformation

And finally, the Word of God is sufficient in social renewal and reform. We are very concerned about this today and rightly so, because we live in a declining culture, and we want to see the lordship of Jesus acknowledged so that justice and true righteousness prevail. We want to see the poor relieved of bitter want and suffering. How is this to happen? Certainly it is not more government programs or increased emphasis on social work, but first of all and above all what is needed is the teaching and practice of the Word of God.

We should remember what happened in Geneva in the sixteenth century through the ministry of John Calvin. In August of 1535 the Council of Two Hundred, governing Geneva, voted to reject Catholicism and align the city with the Protestant Reformation. They had very little idea what this meant. Up to that point the city had been notorious for its riots, gambling, indecent dancing, drunkenness, adultery, and other vices. People would literally run around the streets naked, singing indecent songs and blaspheming God. The people expected this state of affairs to continue, even after they became Protestants. The Council did not know what to do. It passed regulation after regulation designed to restrain the vice and remedy the situation. Nothing worked. Public discipline and morals continued to decline.

Calvin came to Geneva in August of 1536, a year after the change. He was practically ignored. He was not even paid the first year. As everybody knows, his first attempts to preach proved so unpopular he was dismissed by the Council in early 1538 and went to Strasbourg. Calvin was happy in Strasbourg and had no desire to return. But the situation got so bad in Geneva that public opinion turned to him again in desperation. He told his friend William Farel, "I should prefer a hundred other deaths than this cross on which I should have to die a thousand times a day."

Driven by a sense of duty, Calvin returned to Geneva on September 13, 1541. He had no weapon but the Word of God. From the very first his emphasis had been on Bible teaching, and he returned to it now, picking up his exposition of Scripture at precisely the place he had left it three and one half years earlier. He preached from the Word every day, and under the power of his preaching the city changed. As the people of Geneva acquired knowledge of God's Word and allowed it to influence their behavior, the city became almost a New Jerusalem, and the Gospel spread from there to the rest of Europe, Great Britain, and the new world.

Moreover, this change made other changes possible. One student of this historical period writes,

Cleanliness was practically unknown in towns of his generation and epidemics were common and numerous. [Calvin] moved the Council to make permanent regulations for establishing sanitary conditions and supervision of markets. Beggars were prohibited from the streets, but a hospital and poorhouse were provided and well conducted. Calvin labored zealously for the education of all classes and established the famous Academy, whose influence reached all parts of Europe and even to the British Isles. He urged the Council to introduce the cloth and silk industry and thus laid the foundation for the temporal wealth of Geneva. This industry . . . proved especially successful in Geneva because Calvin, through the gospel, created within the individual the love of work, honesty, thrift and cooperation. He taught that capital was not an evil thing, but the blessed result of honest labor and that it could be used for the welfare of mankind. Countries under the influence of Calvinism were invariably connected with growing industry and wealth. . . .

It is no mere coincidence that religious and political liberty arose in those countries where Calvinism had penetrated most deeply, namely, Switzerland, Holland, Germany, Scotland, England, Wales and colonial America.[4]

There has probably never been a clearer example of extensive moral and social reform than this transformation of Geneva under John Calvin, accomplished almost entirely by the preaching of God's Word.

Conclusion

In 2 Timothy 3, Paul encouraged Timothy to continue on the path of ministry he had been walking because "from infancy you have known the holy Scriptures, which are able to make you wise for salvation through faith in Christ Jesus." Why is the Bible able to do this? It is because it is "God-breathed." It is the very Word of God and therefore carries with it the authority and power of God. And it is eminently useful, too. It is useful for "teaching, rebuking, correcting and training in righteousness, so that the man of God may be thoroughly equipped for every good work" (vv. 16–17).

This is what I need. It is what everybody needs. And only the Word of God is sufficient for it.

In summing up, let me offer two final applications. First, if people can only be converted by hearing the gospel message, as Paul says in Romans 10:6–9, 17, then believers must make sure they hear it. It is our responsibility to take the gospel to them and to send others to places where we cannot go ourselves. Do not suppose that what you can do is unimportant or that God is going to save people without human messengers (by a direct word from heaven, for example). All who are saved are saved because Christians have done something to bring the Bible to them.

If you were saved sitting alone in your room, remember that some Christian communicated the message of the Bible to you somehow. It may have been by the direct word of a father or mother, an uncle or a grandmother. It may have been years ago, when you were a child. It may have been more recently. But somehow, some Christian brought you the message about Jesus. Perhaps you did not have exposure to Christian teaching in your family. Perhaps you were converted in a distant city in a lonely hotel room through reading a Gideon Bible. Somebody bought that Bible and somebody else put it there. If you were saved by a tract, some Christian wrote it, others published it, and still others arranged to get it into your hands. The same is true if you have heard the gospel on the radio or on television or through a book.

The Bible says, "Faith comes from hearing the message, and the message is heard through the word of Christ" (Rom. 10:17). That is the way salvation came to you; it is also the way it must go from you to others.

Second, a word for those who are not yet Christians. If you are not yet a believer in Jesus Christ, you need to understand that "faith comes from hearing the message." How do people become believers? By hearing the message. Why is this so? Because the Lord Jesus Christ himself speaks to them through the preacher and calls them to faith.

So take advantage of Bible teaching. Listen to it. Find a faithful pastor who is teaching the Word of God Sunday by Sunday from his pulpit, and learn from him. Open your heart to the words being taught. One commentator wrote, "If you will open your heart now, and willingly pay attention to the good news that God has nothing against you, that he loves you, that he sent the Lord Jesus Christ to die for you, that Christ did die for you personally, and that he was buried, and that God raised him from the dead on the third day as the guarantee of your salvation—if you will open your heart to this, you will find faith coming to you."[5]

"Faith comes from hearing." God has planned it that way. The message is being taught. Open your ears to that truth and trust that, as you do, God will make the message true for you and that you will find yourself calling on the Lord Jesus Christ to be your Savior.

APPENDIX A
THE CHICAGO STATEMENT ON BIBLICAL INERRANCY

The authority of Scripture is a key issue for the Christian church in this and every age. Those who profess faith in Jesus Christ as Lord and Savior are called to show the reality of their discipleship by humbly and faithfully obeying God's written Word. To stray from Scripture in faith or conduct is disloyalty to our Master. Recognition of the total truth and trustworthiness of Holy Scripture is essential to a full grasp and adequate confession of its authority.

The following Statement affirms this inerrancy of Scripture afresh, making clear our understanding of it and warning against its denial. We are persuaded that to deny it is to set aside the witness of Jesus Christ and of the Holy Spirit and to refuse that submission to the claims of God's own Word which marks true Christian faith. We see it as our timely duty to make this affirmation in the face of current lapses from the truth of inerrancy among our fellow Christians and misunderstanding of this doctrine in the world at large.

This Statement consists of three parts: a Summary Statement, Articles of Affirmation and Denial, and an accompanying Exposition. It has been prepared in the course of a three-day consultation in Chicago. Those who have signed the Summary Statement and the Articles wish to affirm their own conviction as to the inerrancy of Scripture and to encourage and challenge one another and all Christians to growing appreciation and understanding of this doctrine. We acknowledge the limitations of a document prepared in a brief, intensive conference and do not propose that this Statement be given creedal weight. Yet we rejoice in the deepening of our own convictions through our discussions together, and we pray that the Statement we have signed may be used to the glory of our God toward a new reformation of the church in its faith, life, and mission.

We offer this Statement in a spirit, not of contention, but of humility and love, which we purpose by God's grace to maintain in any future dialogue arising out of what we have said. We gladly acknowledge that many who deny the inerrancy of Scripture do not display the consequences of this denial in the rest of their belief and behavior, and we are conscious that we who confess this doctrine often deny it in life by failing to bring our thoughts and deeds, our traditions and habits, into true subjection to the divine Word.

We invite response to this statement from any who see reason to amend its affirmations about Scripture by the light of Scripture itself, under whose infallible authority we stand as we speak. We claim no personal infallibility for the witness we bear, and for any help which enables us to strengthen this testimony to God's Word we shall be grateful.

A Short Statement

1. God, who is himself truth and speaks truth only, has inspired Holy Scripture in order thereby to reveal himself to lost mankind through Jesus Christ as Creator and Lord, Redeemer and Judge. Holy Scripture is God's witness to himself.

2. Holy Scripture, being God's own Word, written by men prepared and superintended by his Spirit, is of infallible divine authority in all matters upon which it touches: it is to be believed, as God's instruction, in all that it affirms; obeyed, as God's command, in all that it requires; embraced, as God's pledge, in all that it promises.

3. The Holy Spirit, Scripture's divine author, both authenticates it to us by his inward witness and opens our minds to understand its meaning.

4. Being wholly and verbally God-given, Scripture is without error or fault in all its teaching, no less in what it states about God's acts in creation, about the events of world history, and about its own literary origins under God, than in its witness to God's saving grace in individual lives.

5. The authority of Scripture is inescapably impaired if this total divine inerrancy is in any way limited or disregarded, or made relative to a view of truth contrary to the Bible's own; and such lapses bring serious loss to both the individual and the church.

Articles of Affirmation and Denial

Article I

We *affirm* that the Holy Scriptures are to be received as the authoritative Word of God.

We *deny* that the Scriptures receive their authority from the church, tradition, or any other human source.

Article II

We *affirm* that the Scriptures are the supreme written norm by which God binds the conscience, and that the authority of the church is subordinate to that of Scripture.

We *deny* that church creeds, councils, or declarations have authority greater than or equal to the authority of the Bible.

Article III

We affirm that the written Word in its entirety is revelation given by God.

We deny that the Bible is merely a witness to revelation, or only becomes revelation in encounter, or depends on the responses of men for its validity.

Article IV

We affirm that God who made mankind in his image has used language as a means of revelation.

We deny that human language is so limited by our creatureliness that it is rendered inadequate as a vehicle for divine revelation. We further deny that the corruption of human culture and language through sin has thwarted God's work of inspiration.

Article V

We affirm that God's revelation within the Holy Scriptures was progressive.

We deny that later revelation, which may fulfill earlier revelation, ever corrects or contradicts it. We further deny that any normative revelation has been given since the completion of the New Testament writings.

Article VI

We affirm that the whole of Scripture and all its parts, down to the very words of the original, were given by divine inspiration.

We deny that the inspiration of Scripture can rightly be affirmed of the whole without the parts, or of some parts but not the whole.

Article VII

We affirm that inspiration was the work in which God by his Spirit, through human writers, gave us his Word. The origin of Scripture is divine. The mode of divine inspiration remains largely a mystery to us.

We deny that inspiration can be reduced to human insight, or to heightened states of consciousness of any kind.

Article VIII

We affirm that God in his work of inspiration utilized the distinctive personalities and literary styles of the writers whom he had chosen and prepared.

We deny that God, in causing these writers to use the very words that he chose, overrode their personalities.

Article IX

We affirm that inspiration, though not conferring omniscience, guaranteed true and trustworthy utterance on all matters of which the biblical authors were moved to speak and write.

We deny that the finitude or fallenness of these writers, by necessity or otherwise, introduced distortion or falsehood into God's Word.

Article X

We affirm that inspiration, strictly speaking, applies only to the autographic text of Scripture, which in the providence of God can be ascertained from available manuscripts with great accuracy. We further affirm that copies and translations of Scripture are the Word of God to the extent that they faithfully represent the original.

We deny that any essential element of the Christian faith is affected by the absence of the autographs. We further deny that this absence renders the assertion of biblical inerrancy invalid or irrelevant.

Article XI

We affirm that Scripture, having been given by divine inspiration, is infallible, so that, far from misleading us, it is true and reliable in all the matters it addresses.

We deny that it is possible for the Bible to be at the same time infallible and errant in its assertions. Infallibility and inerrancy may be distinguished, but not separated.

Article XII

We affirm that Scripture in its entirety is inerrant, being free from all falsehood, fraud, or deceit.

We deny that biblical infallibility and inerrancy are limited to spiritual, religious, or redemptive themes, exclusive of assertions in the fields of history and science. We further deny that scientific hypotheses about earth history may properly be used to overturn the teaching of Scripture on creation and the flood.

Article XIII

We affirm the propriety of using inerrancy as a theological term with reference to the complete truthfulness of Scripture.

We deny that it is proper to evaluate Scripture according to standards of truth and error that are alien to its usage or purpose. We further deny that inerrancy is negated by biblical phenomena such as a lack of modern technical precision, irregularities of grammar or spelling, observational descriptions of nature, the reporting of falsehoods, the use of hyperbole and round numbers, the topical arrangement of material, variant selections of material in parallel accounts, or the use of free citations.

Article XIV

We affirm the unity and internal consistency of Scripture.

We deny that alleged errors and discrepancies that have not yet been resolved vitiate the truth claims of the Bible.

Article XV

We affirm that the doctrine of inerrancy is grounded in the teaching of the Bible about inspiration.

We deny that Jesus' teaching about Scripture may be dismissed by appeals to accommodation or to any natural limitation of his humanity.

Article XVI

We affirm that the doctrine of inerrancy has been integral to the Church's faith throughout its history.

We deny that inerrancy is a doctrine invented by scholastic Protestantism, or is a reactionary position postulated in response to negative higher criticism.

Article XVII

We affirm that the Holy Spirit bears witness to the Scriptures, assuring believers of the truthfulness of God's written Word.

We deny that this witness of the Holy Spirit operates in isolation from or against Scripture.

Article XVIII

We affirm that the text of Scripture is to be interpreted by grammatico-historical exegesis, taking account of its literary forms and devices, and that Scripture is to interpret Scripture.

We deny the legitimacy of any treatment of the text or quest for sources lying behind it that leads to relativizing, dehistoricizing, or discounting its teaching, or rejecting its claims to authorship.

Article XIX

We affirm that a confession of the full authority, infallibility, and inerrancy of Scripture is vital to a sound understanding of the whole of the Christian faith. We further affirm that such confession should lead to increasing conformity to the image of Christ.

We deny that such confession is necessary for salvation. However, we further deny that inerrancy can be rejected without grave consequences, both to the individual and to the church.

Exposition

Our understanding of the doctrine of inerrancy must be set in the context of the broader teachings of the Scripture concerning itself. This exposition gives an account of the outline of doctrine from which our summary statement and articles are drawn.

Creation, Revelation, and Inspiration. The Triune God, who formed all things by his creative utterances and governs all things by his Word of decree, made mankind in his own image for a life of communion with himself, on the model of the eternal fellowship of loving communication within the Godhead. As God's image-bearer, man was to hear God's Word addressed to him and to respond in the joy of adoring obedience. Over and above God's self-disclosure in the created order and the sequence of events within it, human beings from Adam on have received verbal messages from him, either directly, as stated in Scripture, or indirectly in the form of part or all of Scripture itself.

When Adam fell, the Creator did not abandon mankind to final judgment but promised salvation and began to reveal himself as Redeemer in a sequence of historical events centering on Abraham's family and culminating in the life, death, resurrection, present heavenly ministry, and promised return of Jesus Christ. Within this frame God has from time to time spoken specific words of judgment and mercy, promise and command, to sinful human beings, so drawing them into a covenant relation of mutual commitment between him and them in which he blesses them with gifts of grace and they bless him in responsive adoration. Moses, whom God used as mediator to carry his words to his people at the time of the Exodus, stands at the head of a long line of prophets in whose mouths and writings God put his words for delivery to Israel. God's purpose in this succession of messages was to maintain his covenant by causing his people to know his name—that is, his nature—and his will both of precept and purpose in the present and for the future. This line of prophetic spokesmen from God came to completion in Jesus Christ, God's incarnate Word, who was himself a prophet—more than a prophet, but not less—and in the apostles and prophets of the first Christian generation. When God's final and climactic message, his word to the world concerning Jesus Christ, had been spoken and elucidated by those in the apostolic circle, the sequence of revealed messages ceased. Henceforth, the church was to live and know God by what he had already said, and said for all time.

At Sinai God wrote the terms of his covenant on tables of stone, as his enduring witness and for lasting accessibility, and throughout the period of prophetic and apostolic revelation he prompted men to write the messages given to and through them, along with celebratory records of his dealings with his people, plus moral reflections on covenant life and forms of praise and prayer for covenant mercy. The theological reality of inspiration in the producing of biblical documents corresponds to that of spoken prophecies: although the human writer's personalities were expressed in what they wrote, the words were divinely constituted. Thus, what Scripture says, God says; its authority is his authority, for he is its ultimate Author, having given it through the minds and words of chosen and prepared men who in freedom and faithfulness "spoke from God as they were carried along by the Holy Spirit" (2 Pet. 1:21). Holy Scripture must be acknowledged as the Word of God by virtue of its divine origin.

Authority: Christ and the Bible. Jesus Christ, the Son of God who is the Word made flesh, our Prophet, Priest, and King, is the ultimate Mediator of God's communication to man, as he is of all God's gifts of grace. The revelation he gave was more than verbal; he revealed the Father by his presence and his deeds as well. Yet his words were crucially important; for he was God, he spoke from the Father, and his words will judge all men at the last day.

As the prophesied Messiah, Jesus Christ is the central theme of Scripture. The Old Testament looked ahead to him; the New Testament looks back to his first coming and on to his second. Canonical Scripture is the divinely inspired and therefore normative witness to Christ. No hermeneutic, therefore, of which the historical Christ is not the focal point is acceptable. Holy

Scripture must be treated as what it essentially is—the witness of the Father to the incarnate Son.

It appears that the Old Testament canon had been fixed by the time of Jesus. The New Testament canon is likewise now closed inasmuch as no new apostolic witness to the historical Christ can now be borne. No new revelation (as distinct from Spirit-given understanding of existing revelation) will be given until Christ comes again. The canon was created in principle by divine inspiration. The church's part was to discern the canon which God had created, not to devise one of its own.

The word *canon*, signifying a rule or standard, is a pointer to authority, which means the right to rule and control. Authority in Christianity belongs to God in his revelation, which means, on the one hand, Jesus Christ, the living Word, and, on the other hand, Holy Scripture, the written Word. But the authority of Christ and that of Scripture are one. As our Prophet, Christ testified that Scripture cannot be broken. As our Priest and King, he devoted his earthly life to fulfilling the law and the prophets, even dying in obedience to the words of Messianic prophecy. Thus, as he saw Scripture attesting him and his authority, so by his own submission to Scripture he attested its authority. As he bowed to his Father's instruction given in his Bible (our Old Testament), so he requires his disciples to do—not, however, in isolation but in conjunction with the apostolic witness to himself which he undertook to inspire by his gift of the Holy Spirit. So Christians show themselves faithful servants of their Lord by bowing to the divine instruction given in the prophetic and apostolic writings which together make up our Bible.

By authenticating each other's authority, Christ and Scripture coalesce into a single fount of authority. The biblically interpreted Christ and the Christ-centered, Christ-proclaiming Bible are from this standpoint one. As from the fact of inspiration we infer that what Scripture says, God says, so from the revealed relation between Jesus Christ and Scripture we may equally declare that what Scripture says, Christ says.

Infallibility, Inerrancy, Interpretation. Holy Scripture, as the inspired Word of God witnessing authoritatively to Jesus Christ, may properly be called *infallible* and *inerrant*. These negative terms have a special value, for they explicitly safeguard crucial positive truths.

Infallible signifies the quality of neither misleading nor being misled and so safeguards in categorical terms the truth that Holy Scripture is a sure, safe, and reliable rule and guide in all matters.

Similarly, *inerrant* signifies the quality of being free from all falsehood or mistake and so safeguards the truth that Holy Scripture is entirely true and trustworthy in all its assertions.

We affirm that canonical Scripture should always be interpreted on the basis that it is infallible and inerrant. However, in determining what the God-taught writer is asserting in each passage, we must pay the most careful attention to its claims and character as a human production. In inspiration, God utilized the culture and conventions of his penman's milieu, a milieu that God controls in his sovereign providence; it is misinterpretation to imagine otherwise.

So history must be treated as history, poetry as poetry, hyperbole and metaphor as hyperbole and metaphor, generalization and approximation as what they are, and so forth. Differences between literary conventions in Bible times and in ours must also be observed: since, for instance, non-chronological narration and imprecise citation were conventional and acceptable and violated no expectations in those days, we must not regard these things as faults when we find them in Bible writers. When total precision of a particular kind was not expected nor aimed at, it is no error not to have achieved it. Scripture is inerrant, not in the sense of being absolutely precise by modern standards, but in the sense of making good its claims and achieving that measure of focused truth at which its authors aimed.

The truthfulness of Scripture is not negated by the appearance in it of irregularities of grammar or spelling, phenomenal descriptions of nature, reports of false statements (*e.g.*, the lies of Satan), or seeming discrepancies between one passage and another. It is not right to set the so-called "phenomena" of Scripture against the teaching of Scripture about itself. Apparent inconsistencies should not be ignored. Solution of them, where this can be convincingly achieved, will encourage our faith, and where for the present no convincing solution is at hand we shall significantly honor God by trusting his assurance that his Word is true, despite these appearances, and by maintaining our confidence that one day they will be seen to have been illusions.

Inasmuch as all Scripture is the product of a single divine mind, interpretation must stay within the bounds of the analogy of Scripture and eschew hypotheses that would correct one biblical passage by another, whether in the name of progressive revelation or of the imperfect enlightenment of the inspired writer's mind.

Although Holy Scripture is nowhere culture-bound in the sense that its teaching lacks universal validity, it is sometimes culturally conditioned by the customs and conventional views of a particular period, so that the application of its principles today calls for a different sort of action.

Skepticism and Criticism. Since the Renaissance, and more particularly since the Enlightenment, world views have been developed which involve skepticism about basic Christian tenets. Such are the agnosticism which denies that God is knowable, the rationalism which denies that he is incomprehensible, the idealism which denies that he is transcendent, and the existentialism which denies rationality in his relationships with us. When these un- and anti-biblical principles seep into men's theologies at a presuppositional level, as today they frequently do, faithful interpretation of Holy Scripture becomes impossible.

Transmission and Translation. Since God has nowhere promised an inerrant transmission of Scripture, it is necessary to affirm that only the autographic text of the original documents was inspired and to maintain the need of textual criticism as a means of detecting any slips that may have crept into the text in the course of its transmission. The verdict of this science, however, is that the Hebrew and Greek text appear to be amazingly well preserved, so that we are amply justified in affirming, with the Westminster Confession, a singular providence of God in this matter and in declaring that the authority of Scripture is in no way jeopardized by the fact that the copies we possess are not entirely error-free.

Similarly, no translation is or can be perfect, and all translations are an additional step away from the *autographa*. Yet the verdict of linguistic science is that English-speaking Christians, at least, are exceedingly well served in these days with a host of excellent translations and have no cause for hesitating to conclude that the true Word of God is within their reach. Indeed, in view of the frequent repetition in Scripture of the main matters with which it deals and also of the Holy Spirit's constant witness to and through the Word, no serious translation of Holy Scripture will so destroy its meaning as to render it unable to make its reader "wise for salvation through faith in Christ Jesus" (2 Tim. 3:15).

Inerrancy and Authority. In our affirmation of the authority of Scripture as involving its total truth, we are consciously standing with Christ and his apostles, indeed with the whole Bible and with the main stream of church history from the first days until very recently. We are concerned at the casual, inadvertent, and seemingly thoughtless way in which a belief of such far-reaching importance has been given up by so many in our day.

We are conscious too that great and grave confusion results from ceasing to maintain the total truth of the Bible whose authority one professes to acknowledge. The result of taking this step is that the Bible which God gave loses its authority, and what has authority instead is a Bible reduced in content according to the demands of one's critical reasonings and in principle reducible still further once one has started. This means that at bottom independent reason now has authority, as opposed to scriptural teaching. If this is not seen and if for the time being basic evangelical doctrines are still held, persons denying the full truth of Scripture may claim an evangelical identity while methodologically they have moved away from the evangelical principle of knowledge to an unstable subjectivism, and will find it hard not to move further.

We affirm that what Scripture says, God says. May he be glorified. Amen and Amen.

APPENDIX B
THE CHICAGO STATEMENT ON BIBLICAL HERMENEUTICS

Summit I of the International Council on Biblical Inerrancy took place in Chicago on October 26–28, 1978, for the purpose of affirming afresh the doctrine of the inerrancy of Scripture, making clear the understanding of it and warning against its denial. In the four years since Summit I, God has blessed that effort in ways surpassing most anticipations. A gratifying flow of helpful literature on the doctrine of inerrancy as well as a growing commitment to its value give cause to pour forth praise to our great God.

The work of Summit I had hardly been completed when it became evident that there was yet another major task to be tackled. While we recognize that belief in the inerrancy of Scripture is basic to maintaining its authority, the values of that commitment are only as real as one's understanding of the meaning of Scripture. Thus, the need for Summit II. For two years plans were laid and papers were written on themes relating to hermeneutical principles and practices. The culmination of this effort has been a meeting in Chicago on November 10–13, 1982, at which we, the undersigned, have participated.

In similar fashion to the Chicago Statement of 1978, we herewith present these affirmations and denials as an expression of the results of our labors to clarify hermeneutical issues and principles. We do not claim completeness or systematic treatment of the entire subject, but these affirmations and denials represent a consensus of the approximately one hundred participants and observers gathered at this conference. It has been a broadening experience to engage in dialogue, and it is our prayer that God will use the product of our diligent efforts to enable us and others to more correctly handle the word of truth (2 Tim. 2:15).

Articles of Affirmation and Denial

Article I

We *affirm* that the normative authority of Holy Scripture is the authority of God himself, and is attested by Jesus Christ, the Lord of the Church.

We *deny* the legitimacy of separating the authority of Christ from the authority of Scripture, or of opposing the one to the other.

Article II

We *affirm* that as Christ is God and man in one person, so Scripture is, indivisibly, God's Word in human language.

We *deny* that the humble, human form of Scripture entails errancy any more than the humanity of Christ, even in his humiliation, entails sin.

Article III

We *affirm* that the person and work of Jesus Christ are the central focus of the entire Bible.

We *deny* that any method of interpretation which rejects or obscures the Christ-centeredness of Scripture is correct.

Article IV

We affirm that the Holy Spirit who inspired Scripture acts through it today to work faith in its message.

We deny that the Holy Spirit ever teaches to any one anything which is contrary to the teaching of Scripture.

Article V

We affirm that the Holy Spirit enables believers to appropriate and apply Scripture to their lives.

We deny that the natural man is able to discern spiritually the biblical message apart from the Holy Spirit.

Article VI

We affirm that the Bible expresses God's truth in propositional statements, and we declare that biblical truth is both objective and absolute. We further affirm that a statement is true if it represents matters as they actually are, but is an error if it misrepresents the facts.

We deny that, while Scripture is able to make us wise unto salvation, biblical truth should be defined in terms of this function. We further deny that error should be defined as that which willfully deceives.

Article VII

We affirm that the meaning expressed in each biblical text is single, definite, and fixed.

We deny that the recognition of this single meaning eliminates the variety of its application.

Article VIII

We affirm that the Bible contains teachings and mandates which apply to all cultural and situational contexts and other mandates which the Bible itself shows apply only to particular situations.

We deny that the distinction between the universal and particular mandates of Scripture can be determined by cultural and situational factors. We further deny that universal mandates may ever be treated as culturally or situationally relative.

Article IX

We affirm that the term hermeneutics, which historically signified the rules of exegesis, may properly be extended to cover all that is involved in the process of perceiving what the biblical revelation means and how it bears on our lives.

We deny that the message of Scripture derives from, or is dictated by, the interpreter's understanding. Thus we deny that the "horizons" of the biblical writer and the interpreter may rightly "fuse" in such a way that what the text communicates to the interpreter is not ultimately controlled by the expressed meaning of the Scripture.

Article X

We affirm that Scripture communicates God's truth to us verbally through a wide variety of literary forms.

We deny that any of the limits of human language render Scripture inadequate to convey God's message.

Article XI

We affirm that translations of the text of Scripture can communicate knowledge of God across all temporal and cultural boundaries.

We deny that the meaning of biblical texts is so tied to the culture out of which they came that understanding of the same meaning in other cultures is impossible.

Article XII

We affirm that in the task of translating the Bible and teaching it in the context of each culture, only those functional equivalents which are faithful to the content of biblical teaching should be employed.

We deny the legitimacy of methods which either are insensitive to the demands of cross-cultural communication or distort biblical meaning in the process.

Article XIII

We affirm that awareness of the literary categories, formal and stylistic, of the various parts of Scripture is essential for proper exegesis, and hence we value genre criticism as one of the many disciplines of biblical study.

We deny that generic categories which negate historicity may rightly be imposed on biblical narratives which present themselves as factual.

Article XIV

We affirm that the biblical record of events, discourses and sayings, though presented in a variety of appropriate literary forms, corresponds to historical fact.

We deny that any event, discourse, or saying reported in Scripture was invented by the biblical writers or by the traditions they incorporated.

Article XV

We affirm the necessity of interpreting the Bible according to its literal, or normal, sense. The literal sense is the grammatical-historical sense, that is, the meaning which the writer expressed. Interpretation according to the literal sense will take account of all figures of speech and literary forms found in the text.

We deny the legitimacy of any approach to Scripture that attributes to it meaning which the literal sense does not support.

Article XVI

We affirm that legitimate critical techniques should be used in determining the canonical text and its meaning.

We deny the legitimacy of allowing any method of biblical criticism to question the truth or integrity of the writer's expressed meaning, or of any other scriptural teaching.

Article XVII

We affirm the unity, harmony, and consistency of Scripture and declare that it is its own best interpreter.

We deny that Scripture may be interpreted in such a way as to suggest that one passage corrects or militates against another. We deny that later writers of Scripture misinterpreted earlier passages of Scripture when quoting from or referring to them.

Article XVIII

We affirm that the Bible's own interpretation of itself is always correct, never deviating from, but rather elucidating, the single meaning of the inspired text. The single meaning of a prophet's words includes, but is not restricted to, the understanding of those words by the prophet and necessarily involves the intention of God evidenced in the fulfillment of those words.

We deny that the writers of Scripture always understood the full implications of their own words.

Article XIX

We affirm that any preunderstandings which the interpreter brings to Scripture should be in harmony with scriptural teaching and subject to correction by it.

We deny that Scripture should be required to fit alien preunderstandings inconsistent with itself, such as naturalism, evolutionism, scientism, secular humanism, and relativism.

Article XX

We affirm that since God is the author of all truth, all truths, biblical and extrabiblical, are consistent and cohere, and that the Bible speaks truth when it touches on matters pertaining to nature, history, or anything else. We further affirm that in some cases extrabiblical data have value for clarifying what Scripture teaches, and for prompting correction of faulty interpretations.

We deny that extrabiblical views ever disprove the teaching of Scripture or hold priority over it.

Article XXI

We affirm the harmony of special with general revelation and therefore of biblical teaching with the facts of nature.

We deny that any genuine scientific facts are inconsistent with the true meaning of any passage of Scripture.

Article XXII

We affirm that Genesis 1–11 is factual, as is the rest of the book.

We deny that the teachings of Genesis 1–11 are mythical and that scientific hypotheses about earth history or the origin of humanity may be invoked to overthrow what Scripture teaches about creation.

Article XXIII

We affirm the clarity of Scripture and specifically of its message about salvation from sin.

We deny that all passages of Scripture are equally clear or have equal bearing on the message of redemption.

Article XXIV

We affirm that a person is not dependent for understanding of Scripture on the expertise of biblical scholars.

We deny that a person should ignore the fruits of the technical study of Scripture by biblical scholars.

Article XXV

We affirm that the only type of preaching which sufficiently conveys the divine revelation and its proper application to life is that which faithfully expounds the text of Scripture as the Word of God.

We deny that the preacher has any message from God apart from the text of Scripture.

Exposition

The following paragraphs outline the general theological understanding which the Chicago Statement on Biblical Hermeneutics reflects. They were first drafted as a stimulus toward that statement. They have now been revised in the light of it and of many specific suggestions received during the scholars' conference at which it was drawn up. Though the revision could not be completed in time to present to the conference, there is every reason to regard its substance as expressing with broad accuracy the common mind of the signatories of the statement.

Standpoint of the Exposition. The living God, Creator and Redeemer, is a communicator, and the inspired and inerrant Scriptures which set before us his saving revelation in history are his means of communicating with us today. He who once spoke to the world through Jesus Christ his Son speaks to us still in and through his written Word. Publicly and privately, therefore, through preaching, personal study, and meditation, with prayer and in the fellowship of the body of Christ, Christian people must continually labor to interpret the Scriptures so that their normative divine message to us may be properly understood. To have formulated the biblical concept of Scripture as authoritative revelation in writing, the God-given rule of faith and life, will be of no profit where the message of Scripture is not rightly grasped and applied. So it is of vital importance to detect and dismiss defective ways of interpreting what is written and to replace them with faithful interpretation of God's infallible Word.

That is the purpose this exposition seeks to serve. What it offers is basic perspectives on the hermeneutical task in the light of three convictions. First, Scripture, being God's own instruction to us, is abidingly true and utterly trustworthy. Second, hermeneutics is crucial to the battle for biblical authority in the contemporary church. Third, as knowledge of the inerrancy of Scripture must control interpretation, forbidding us to discount anything that Scripture proves to affirm, so interpretation must clarify the scope and significance of that inerrancy by determining what affirmations Scripture actually makes.

The Communication between God and Mankind. God has made mankind in his own image, personal and rational, for eternal loving fellowship with himself in a communion that rests on two-way communication: God addressing to us words of revelation and we answering him in words of prayer and praise. God's gift of language was given us partly to make possible these interchanges and partly also that we might share our understanding of God with others.

In testifying to the historical process from Adam to Christ whereby God re-established fellowship with our fallen race, Scripture depicts him as constantly using his own gift of language to send men messages about what he would do and what they should do. The God of the Bible uses many forms of speech: he narrates, informs, instructs, warns, reasons, promises, commands, explains, exclaims, entreats, and encourages. The God who saves is also the God who speaks in all these ways.

Biblical writers, historians, prophets, poets, and teachers alike, cite Scripture as God's word of address to all its readers and hearers. To regard Scripture as the Creator's present personal invitation to fellowship, setting standards for faith and godliness not only for its own time but for all time, is integral to biblical faith.

Though God is revealed in the natural order, in the course of history, and in the deliverances of conscience, sin makes mankind impervious and unresponsive to this general revelation. And general revelation is in any case only a disclosure of the Creator as the world's good Lord and just Judge; it does not tell of salvation through Jesus Christ. To know about the Christ of Scripture is thus a necessity for that knowledge of God and communion with him to which he calls sinners today. As the biblical message is heard, read, preached, and taught, the Holy Spirit works with and through it to open the eyes of the spiritually blind and to instill this knowledge.

God has caused Scripture so to be written, and the Spirit so ministers with it, that all who read it, humbly seeking God's help, will be able to understand its saving message. The Spirit's ministry does not make needless the discipline of personal study but rather makes it effective.

To deny the rational, verbal, cognitive character of God's communication to us, to posit an antithesis as some do between revelation as personal and as propositional, and to doubt the adequacy of language as we have it to bring God's authentic message are fundamental mistakes. The humble verbal form of biblical language no more invalidates it as revelation of God's mind than the humble servant-form of the Word made flesh invalidates the claim that Jesus truly reveals the Father.

To deny that God has made plain in Scripture as much as each human being needs to know for his or her spiritual welfare would be a further mistake. Any obscurities we find in Scripture are not intrinsic to it but reflect our own limitations of information and insight. Scripture is clear and sufficient both as a source of doctrine, binding the conscience, and as a guide to eternal life and godliness, shaping our worship and service of the God who creates, loves, and saves.

The Authority of Scripture. Holy Scripture is the self-revelation of God in and through the words of men. It is both their witness to God and God's witness to himself. As the divine-human record and interpretation of God's redemptive work in history, it is cognitive revelation, truth addressed to our minds for understanding and response. God is its source, and Jesus Christ, the Savior, is its center of reference and main subject matter. Its absolute and abiding worth as an infallible directive for faith and living follows from its God-givenness (cf. 2 Tim. 3:15–17). Being as fully divine as it is human, it expresses God's wisdom in all its teaching and speaks reliably—that is, infallibly and inerrantly—in every informative assertion it makes. It is a set of occasional writings, each with its own specific character and content, which together constitute an organism of universally relevant truth, namely, bad news about universal human sin and need answered by good news about a particular first-century Jew who is shown to be the Son of God and the world's only Savior. The volume which these constituent books make is as broad as life and bears upon every human problem and aspect of behavior. In setting before us the history of redemption—the law and the gospel, God's commands, promises, threats, works, and ways, and object lessons concerning faith and obedience and their opposites, with their respective outcomes—Scripture shows us the entire panorama of human existence as God wills us to see it.

The authority of Holy Scripture is bound up with the authority of Jesus Christ, whose recorded words express the principle that the teaching of Israel's Scriptures (our Old Testament), together with his own teaching and the witness of the apostles (our New Testament), constitute his appointed rule of faith and conduct for his followers. He did not criticize his Bible, though he criticized misinterpretations of it; on the contrary, he affirmed its binding authority over him and all his disciples (cf. Matt. 5:17–19). To separate the authority of Christ from that of Scripture and to oppose the one to the other are thus mistakes. To oppose the authority of one apostle to that of another or the teaching of an apostle at one time to that of his teaching at another time are mistakes also.

The Holy Spirit and the Scriptures. The Holy Spirit of God, who moved the human authors to produce the biblical books, now accompanies them with his power. He led the church to discern their inspiration in the canonizing process; he continually confirms this discernment to individuals through the unique impact which he causes Scripture to make upon them. He helps them as they study, pray, meditate, and seek to learn in the church, to understand and commit themselves to those things which the Bible teaches, and to know the living triune God whom the Bible presents.

The Spirit's illumination can only be expected where the biblical text is diligently studied. Illumination does not yield new truth, over and above what the Bible says; rather, it enables us to see what Scripture was showing us all along. Illumination binds our consciences to Scripture as God's Word and brings joy and worship as we find the Word yielding up to us its meaning. By contrast, intellectual and emotional impulses to disregard or quarrel with the teaching of Scripture come not from the Spirit of God but from some other source. Demonstrable misunderstandings and misinterpretations of Scripture may not be ascribed to the Spirit's leading.

The Idea of Hermeneutics. Biblical hermeneutics has traditionally been understood as the study of right principles for understanding the biblical text. "Understanding" may stop short at a theoretical and notional level, or it may advance via the assent and commitment of faith to become experiential through personal acquaintance with the God to whom the theories and notions refer. Theoretical understanding of Scripture requires of us no more than is called for to comprehend any ancient literature, that is, sufficient knowledge of the language and background and sufficient empathy with the different cultural context. But there is no experiential understanding of Scripture—no personal knowledge of the God to whom it points—without the Spirit's illumination. Biblical hermeneutics studies the way in which both levels of understanding are attained.

The Scope of Biblical Interpretation. The interpreter's task in broadest definition is to understand both what Scripture meant historically and what it means for us today, that is, how it bears on our lives. This task involves three constant activities.

First comes *exegesis*, the extracting from the text of what God by the human writer was expressing to the latter's envisaged readers.

Second comes *integration*, the correlating of what each exegetical venture has yielded with whatever other biblical teaching bears on the matter in hand and with the rest of biblical teaching as such. Only within this frame of reference can the full meaning of the exegeted teaching be determined.

Third comes *application* of the exegeted teaching, viewed explicitly as God's teaching, for the correcting and directing of thought and action. Application is based on the knowledge that God's character and will, man's nature and need, the saving ministry of Jesus Christ, the experiential aspects of godliness including the common life of the church and the many-sided relationship between God and his world including his plan for its history are realities which do not change with the passing years. It is with these matters that both testaments constantly deal.

Interpretation and application of Scripture take place most naturally in preaching, and all preaching should be based on this threefold procedure. Otherwise, biblical teaching will be misunderstood and misapplied, and confusion and ignorance regarding God and his ways will result.

Formal Rules of Biblical Interpretation. The faithful use of reason in biblical interpretation is ministerial, not magisterial; the believing interpreter will use his mind not to impose or manufacture meaning but to grasp the meaning that is already there in the material itself. The work of scholars who, though not themselves Christians, have been able to understand biblical ideas accurately will be a valuable resource in the theoretical part of the interpreter's task.

a. Interpretation should adhere to the *literal* sense, that is, the single literary meaning which each passage carries. The initial quest is always for what God's penman meant by what he wrote. The discipline of interpretation excludes all attempts to go behind the text, just as it excludes all reading into passages of meanings which cannot be read out of them and all pursuit of ideas sparked off in us by the text which do not arise as part of the author's own expressed flow of thought. Symbols and figures of speech must be recognized for what they are, and arbitrary allegorizing (as distinct from the drawing out of typology which was demonstrably in the writer's mind) must be avoided.

b. The literal sense of each passage should be sought by *the grammatical-historical method,* that is, by asking what is the linguistically natural way to understand the text in its historical setting. Textual, historical, literary, and theological study, aided by linguistic skills—philological, semantic, logical—is the way forward here. Passages should be exegeted in the context of the book of which they are part, and the quest for the writer's own meaning, as distinct from that of his known or supposed sources, must be constantly pursued. The legitimate use of the various critical disciplines is not to call into question the integrity or truth of the writer's meaning but simply to help us determine it.

c. Interpretation should adhere to the principle of *harmony* in the biblical material. Scripture exhibits a wide diversity of concepts and viewpoints within a common faith and an advancing disclosure of divine truth within the biblical period. These differences should not be minimized, but the unity which underlies the diversity should not be lost sight of at any point. We should look to Scripture to interpret Scripture and deny as a matter of method that particular texts, all of which have the one Holy Spirit as their source, can be genuinely discrepant with each other. Even when we cannot at present demonstrate their harmony in a convincing way, we should proceed on the basis that they are in fact harmonious and that fuller knowledge will show this.

d. Interpretation should be *canonical,* that is, the teaching of the Bible as a whole should always be viewed as providing the framework within which our understanding of each particular passage must finally be reached and into which it must finally be fitted.

Valuable as an aid in determining the literal meaning of biblical passages is the discipline of genre criticism, which seeks to identify in terms of style, form and content, the various literary categories to which the biblical books and particular passages within them belong. The literary genre in which each writer creates his text belongs in part at least to his own culture and will be clarified through knowledge of that culture. Since mistakes about genre lead to large-scale misunderstandings of biblical material, it is important that this particular discipline not be neglected.

The Centrality of Jesus Christ in the Biblical Message. Jesus Christ and the saving grace of God in him are the central themes of the Bible. Both Old and New Testaments bear witness to Christ, and the New Testament interpretation of the Old Testament points to him consistently. Types and prophecies in the Old Testament anticipated his coming, his atoning death, his resurrection, his reign, and his return. The office and ministry of priests, prophets and kings, the divinely instituted ritual and sacrificial offerings, and the patterns of redemptive action in Old Testament history, all had typical significance as foreshadowings of Jesus. Old Testament believers looked forward to his coming and lived and were saved by faith which had Christ and his kingdom in view, just as Christians today are saved by faith in Christ, the Savior, who died for our sins and who now lives and reigns and will one day return. That the church and kingdom of Jesus Christ are central to the plan of God which Scripture reveals is not open to question, though opinions divide as to the precise way in which church and kingdom relate to each other. Any way of interpreting Scripture which misses its consistent Christ-centeredness must be judged erroneous.

Biblical and Extra-Biblical Knowledge. Since all facts cohere, the truth about them must be coherent also; and since God, the author of all Scripture, is also the Lord of all facts, there can in principle be no contradiction between a right understanding of what Scripture says and a right account of any reality or event in the created order. Any appearance of contradiction here would argue misunderstanding or inadequate knowledge, either of what Scripture really affirms or of what the extra-biblical facts really are. Thus it would be a summons to reassessment and further scholarly inquiry.

Biblical Statements and Natural Science. What the Bible says about the facts of nature is as true and trustworthy as anything else it says. However, it speaks of natural phenomena as they are spoken of in ordinary language, not in the explanatory technical terms of modern science; it accounts for natural events in terms of the action of God, not in terms of causal links within the created order; and it often describes natural processes figuratively and poetically, not analytically and prosaically as modern science seeks to do. This being so, differences of opinion as to the correct scientific account to give of natural facts and events which Scripture celebrates can hardly be avoided.

It should be remembered, however, that Scripture was given to reveal God, not to address scientific issues in scientific terms, and that, as it does not use the language of modern science, so it does not require scientific knowledge about the internal processes of God's creation for the understanding of its essential message about God and ourselves. Scripture interprets scientific knowledge by relating it to the revealed purpose and work of God, thus establishing an ultimate context for the study and reform of scientific ideas. It is not for scientific theories to dictate what Scripture may and may not say, although extra-biblical information will sometimes helpfully expose a misinterpretation of Scripture.

In fact, interrogating biblical statements about nature in the light of scientific knowledge about their subject matter may help toward attaining a more precise exegesis of them. For although exegesis must be controlled by the text itself, not shaped by extraneous considerations, the exegetical process is constantly stimulated by questioning the text as to whether it means this or that.

Norm and Culture in the Biblical Revelation. As we find in Scripture unchanging truths about God and his will expressed in a variety of verbal forms, so we find them applied in a variety of cultural and situational contexts. Not all biblical teaching about conduct is normative for behavior today. Some applications of moral principles are restricted to a limited audience, the nature and extent of which Scripture itself specifies. One task of exegesis is to distinguish these absolute and normative truths from those aspects of their recorded application which are relative to changing situations. Only when this distinction is drawn can we hope to see how the same absolute truths apply to us in our own culture.

To fail to see how a particular application of an absolute principle has been culturally determined (for instance, as most would agree, Paul's command that Christians greet each other with a kiss) and to treat a revealed absolute as culturally relative (for instance, as again most would agree, God's prohibition in the Pentateuch of homosexual activity) would both be mistakes. Though cultural developments, including conventional values and latter-day social change, may legitimately challenge traditional ways of applying biblical principles, they may not be used either to modify those principles in themselves or to evade their application altogether.

In cross-cultural communication a further step must be taken: the Christian teacher must re-apply revealed absolutes to persons living in a culture that is not the teacher's own. The demands of this task highlight the importance of his being clear on what is absolute in the biblical presentation of the will and work of God and what is a culturally-relative application of it. Engaging in the task may help him toward clarity at this point by making him more alert than before to the presence in Scripture of culturally-conditioned applications of truth, which have to be adjusted according to the cultural variable.

Encountering God through His Word. The twentieth century has seen many attempts to assert the instrumentality of Scripture in bringing to us God's Word while yet denying that that Word has been set forth for all time in the words of the biblical text. These views regard the text as the fallible human witness by means of which God fashions and prompts those insights which he gives us through preaching and Bible study. But for the most part these views include a denial that the Word of God is cognitive communication, and thus they lapse inescapably into impressionistic mysticism. Also, their denial that Scripture is the objectively given Word of God makes the relation of that Word to the text indefinable and hence permanently problematical. This is true of all current forms of neo-orthodox and existentialist theology, including the so-called "new hermeneutic," which is an extreme and incoherent version of the approach described.

The need to appreciate the cultural differences between our world and that of the biblical writers and to be ready to find that God through his Word is challenging the presuppositions and limitations of our present outlook, are two emphases currently associated with the "new hermeneutic." But both really belong to the understanding of the interpretative task which this exposition has set out.

The same is true of the emphasis laid in theology of the existentialist type on the reality of a transforming encounter with God and his Son, Jesus Christ, through the Scriptures. Certainly, the crowning glory of the Scriptures is that they do in fact mediate life-giving fellowship with God incarnate, the living Christ of whom they testify, the divine Savior whose words "are spirit and . . . are life" (John 6:63). But there is no Christ save the Christ of the Bible, and only to the extent that the Bible's presentation of Jesus and of God's plan centering upon him is trusted can genuine spiritual encounter with Jesus Christ ever be expected to take place. It is by means of disciplined interpretations of a trusted Bible that the Father and Son, through the Spirit, make themselves known to sinful men. To such transforming encounters the hermeneutical principles and procedures stated here both mark and guard the road.

J. I. Packer

APPENDIX C
THE CHICAGO STATEMENT ON BIBLICAL APPLICATION

This statement is the third and final in a trilogy of Summits sponsored by the International Council on Biblical Inerrancy. Summit I (October 26–28, 1978) produced the Chicago Statement on Biblical Inerrancy. Summit II (November 10–13, 1982) resulted in the Chicago Statement on Biblical Hermeneutics. This last conference, Summit III (December 10–13, 1986), drafted the Chicago Statement on Biblical Application. With this statement the proposed scholarly work of ICBI has been completed, for the doctrine of inerrancy has thus been defined, interpreted, and applied by many of the leading evangelical scholars of our day.

Note

The participants at Summit III signed the following State-ment of Affirmations and Denials with the following preface:

"As a participant in Summit III of ICBI, I subscribe to these articles as an expression of my agreement of their overall thrust."

Articles of Affirmation and Denial

Article I: The Living God

We affirm that the one true and living God is the creator and sustainer of all things.

We affirm that this God can be known through his revelation of himself in his inerrant Word.

We affirm that this one God exists eternally in three persons, Father, Son, and Holy Spirit, each of whom is fully God.

We affirm that this living, acting, speaking God entered into history through the Son Jesus Christ to bring salvation to the human race.

We affirm that the revealed character and will of God are the foundation of all morality.

We deny that the human language of Scripture is inadequate to inform us who God is or what he is like.

We deny that the doctrine of the Trinity is a contradiction or is based upon an unacceptable ontology.

We deny that the notion of God should be accommodated to modern thought which has no place for the concepts of sin and salvation.

Article II: The Savior and His Work

We affirm that Jesus Christ is true God, begotten from the Father from all eternity, and also true man, conceived by the Holy Spirit and born of the virgin Mary.

We affirm that the indivisible union of full deity with full humanity in the one person of Jesus Christ is essential for his saving work.

We affirm that Jesus Christ, through his vicarious suffering, death, and resurrection, is the only Savior and Redeemer of the world.

We affirm that salvation is by faith alone in Jesus Christ alone.

We affirm that Jesus Christ, as revealed in Scripture, is the supreme model of the godly life that is ours in and through him.

We deny that Scripture warrants any proclamation or offer of salvation except on the basis of the saving work of the crucified and risen Christ.

We deny that those who die without Christ can be saved in the life to come.

We deny that persons capable of rational choice can be saved without personal faith in the biblical Christ.

We deny that presenting Jesus Christ as a moral example without reference to his deity and substitutionary atonement does justice to the teaching of Scripture.

We deny that a proper understanding of the love and justice of God warrants the hope of universal salvation.

Article III: The Holy Spirit and His Work

We affirm that the Holy Spirit is the third person of the Triune Godhead and that his work is essential for the salvation of sinners.

We affirm that true and saving knowledge of God is given by the Spirit of God as he authenticates and illuminates the Word of canonical Scripture, of which he is the primary author.

We affirm that the Holy Spirit guides the people of God, giving them wisdom to apply Scripture to modern issues and everyday life.

We affirm that the church's vitality in worship and fellowship, its faithfulness in confession, its fruitfulness in witness, and its power in mission, depend directly on the power of the Holy Spirit.

We deny that any view that disputes the essential tripersonality of the one God is compatible with the gospel.

We deny that any person can say from the heart that Jesus is Lord apart from the Holy Spirit.

We deny that the Holy Spirit, since the apostolic age, has ever given, or does now give, new normative revelation to the church.

We deny that the name of renewal should be given to any movement in the church that does not involve a deepened sense of God's judgment and mercy in Christ.

Article IV: The Church and Its Mission

We affirm that the inspiration of the Holy Spirit gives the Bible its canonical authority, and the role of the church was and is to recognize and affirm this authority.

We affirm that Christ the Lord has established his church on earth and rules it by his Word and Spirit.

We affirm that the church is apostolic as it receives and is established upon the doctrine of the apostles recorded in Scripture and continues to proclaim the apostolic gospel.

We affirm that identifying marks of local churches are faithful confession and proclamation of the Word of God, and responsible administration of baptism and the Lord's Supper.

We affirm that churches are subject to the Word of Christ in their order as in their doctrine.

We affirm that in addition to their commitment to a local church, Christians may properly involve themselves in parachurch organizations for specialized ministry.

We affirm that Christ calls the church to serve him by its worship, nurture, and witness as his people in the world.

We affirm that Christ sends the church into the whole world to summon sinful humanity to faith, repentance, and righteousness.

We affirm that the unity and clarity of Scripture encourage us to seek to resolve doctrinal differences among Christians, and so to manifest the oneness of the church in Christ.

We deny that the church can grant canonical authority to Scripture.

We deny that the church is constituted by the will and traditions of men.

We deny that the church can bind the conscience apart from the Word of God.

We deny that the church can free itself from the authority of the written Word of God and still exercise valid discipline in Christ's name.

We deny that the church can accommodate itself to the demands of a particular culture if those demands conflict with scriptural revelation, or if they restrain the liberty of Christian conscience.

We deny that differing cultural situations invalidate the biblical principle of male-female equality or the biblical requirements for their roles in the church.

Article V: Sanctity of Human Life

We affirm that God the Creator is sovereign over all human life and mankind is responsible under God to preserve and protect it.

We affirm that the sanctity of human life is based on the creation of mankind in the image and likeness of God.

We affirm that the life of a human being begins at conception (fertilization) and continues until biological death; thus, abortion (except where the continuance of the pregnancy imminently threatens the mother's physical life), infanticide, suicide, and euthanasia are forms of murder.

We affirm that the penal view of social justice is compatible with the sanctity of human life.

We affirm that withholding food or water in order to cause or hasten death is a violation of the sanctity of life.

We affirm that because advancing medical technology has obscured the distinction between life and death, it is essential to evaluate each terminal case with the greatest care so as to preserve the sanctity of human life.

We deny that the quality of human life has priority over its sanctity.

We deny that the sanctity of pre-natal life negates the propriety of necessary medical procedures to preserve the life of the pregnant mother.

We deny that killing in self-defense, in state-administered capital punishment, or in wars justly fought, is necessarily a violation of the sanctity of human life.

We deny that those who reject a divine basis for moral law are exempt from the ethical and social obligation to preserve and protect innocent human life.

We deny that allowing death without medical intervention to prolong life is always a violation of the sanctity of human life.

Article VI: Marriage and the Family

We affirm that the purpose of marriage is to glorify God and extend his Kingdom on earth in an institution that provides for chastity, companionship, procreation and Christian upbringing of children.

We affirm that since marriage is a sacred covenant under God uniting a man and a woman as one flesh, church and state should require faithfulness to God's intention that it be a permanent bond.

We affirm that in the marriage pattern ordained by God, the husband as head is the loving servant-leader of his wife, and the wife as helper in submissive companionship is a full partner with her husband.

We affirm that loving nurture and discipline of children is a God-ordained duty of parents, and God-ordained obedience to parents is a duty of children.

We affirm that the church has the responsibility to nurture the family.

We affirm that honor to parents is a life-long duty of all persons and includes responsibility for the care of the aged.

We affirm that the family should perform many services now commonly assumed by the state.

We deny that pleasure and self-fulfillment are the basis of marriage and that hardships are justifiable cause for breaking the marriage covenant.

We deny that the biblical ideal of marriage can be fulfilled either by a couple living together without a lawful marriage covenant or by any form of same-sex or group cohabitation.

We deny that the state has the right to legitimize views of marriage and the family unit that contravene biblical standards.

We deny that changing social conditions ever make God-ordained marriage or family roles obsolete or irrelevant.

We deny that the state has the right to usurp biblically designated parental responsibility.

Article VII: Divorce and Remarriage

We affirm that the marriage of Adam and Eve as a lifelong monogamous relationship is the pattern for all marriages within the human race.

We affirm that God unites husband and wife in every covenanted and consummated marriage, and will hold covenant-breakers morally accountable.

We affirm that since the essence of the marriage covenant is life-long commitment to the covenant partner, action in relation to a marital breakdown should at least initially aim at the reconciliation of the partners and restoration of the marriage.

We affirm that God hates divorce, however motivated.

We affirm that although God hates divorce, in a sinful world separation is sometimes advisable and divorce is sometimes inevitable.

We affirm that God forgives repentant sinners, even those who have sinned by sundering their marriages.

We affirm that the local church has the responsibility to discipline those who violate the biblical standards for marriage, compassionately restore those who repent, and faithfully minister God's grace to those whose lives have been scarred by marital disruption.

We deny that any contradiction exists within Scripture on the subject of divorce and remarriage.

We deny that it is sinful to separate or live apart from a promiscuous or abusive spouse.

Article VIII: Sexual Deviations

We affirm that Scripture reveals God's standards for sexual relationships, deviation from which is sinful.

We affirm that sexual intercourse is legitimate only in a heterosexual marriage relationship.

We affirm that God's grace in Christ can deliver men and women from bondage to deviant sexual practice, be they heterosexual or homosexual, and the church must assume responsibility for restoring such members to a life that honors God.

We affirm that God loves homosexuals as well as other sinners, and that homosexual temptations can be resisted in the power of Christ to the glory of his grace, just as other temptations can.

We affirm that Christians must exercise a compassion, kindness, and forgiveness in the ministry of God's grace to those whose lives have been scarred by sexual deviations.

We affirm that human fulfillment does not depend on satisfying sexual drives; hedonism and related philosophies encouraging promiscuous sexuality are wrong and lead to ruin.

We affirm that pornography threatens the well-being of individuals, families, and entire societies, and that it is incumbent upon Christians to seek to check its production and distribution.

We deny that homosexual practice can ever please God.

We deny that heredity, childhood conditioning, or other environmental influences can excuse deviant sexual behavior.

We deny that the sexual molestation or exploitation of children in general and incestuous relationships in particular can ever be justified.

We deny that it is hopeless to look for deliverance from homosexual practices or other forms of sexual deviancy.

We deny that the healing of sexual deviancy is aided by condemnation without compassion or by compassion without the application of Scriptural truth, in confident hope.

Article IX: The State Under God

We affirm that God established civil government as an instrument of his common grace, to restrain sin, to maintain order, and to promote civil justice and general well-being.

We affirm that God gives civil governments the right to use coercive force for the defense and encouragement of those who do good and for the just punishment of those who do evil.

We affirm that it is proper and desirable that Christians take part in civil government and advocate the enactment of laws for the common good in accordance with God's moral law.

We affirm that it is the duty of Christian people to pray for civil authorities and to obey them, except when such obedience would involve the violation of God's moral law or neglect the God-ordained responsibilities of Christian witness.

We affirm that governments have a responsibility before God to establish and enforce laws that accord with God's moral law as it pertains to human relations.

We affirm that Christ's rule of the church through his Word must not be confused with the power he grants to civil governments; such confusion will compromise the purity of the gospel and will violate the conscience of individuals.

We affirm that when families or churches neglect their biblically defined duties, thus jeopardizing the well-being of their members, the state may rightfully intervene.

We deny that the state has the right to usurp authority of other God-given spheres of life, especially in the church and in the family.

We deny that the Kingdom of God can be established by the coercive power of civil governments.

We deny that the state has the right to forbid voluntary prayer and other voluntary religious exercises at an appropriate time in the public school.

We deny that God's providential establishment of a particular government confers special blessing, apart from the government's just and faithful execution of its duties.

We deny that religious belief is an essential prerequisite to service in civil government, or that its absence invalidates the legal authority of those who govern.

We deny that the Kingdom of God can be established by the power of civil governments.

We deny that the government has the right to prescribe specific prayers or forms of religious exercise for its citizens.

Article X: Law and Justice

We affirm that the Scriptures are the only infallible record of unchanging moral principles basic to a sound jurisprudence and an adequate philosophy of human rights.

We affirm that God has impressed his image on the hearts of all people so that they are morally accountable to him for their actions as individuals and as members of society.

We affirm that God's revealed law, the moral nature of mankind, and human legislation serve to restrain the fallen political order from chaos and anarchy and to point humankind to the need for redemption in Jesus Christ.

We affirm that the Gospel cannot be legislated and the Law cannot save sinners.

We deny that legal positivism, or any other humanistic philosophy of law, is able to satisfy the need for absolute standards of law and justice.

We deny that any person or any society fulfills God's standards so as to justify himself, herself, or itself before the tribunal of God's absolute justice.

We deny that any political, economic, or social order is free from the deadly consequences of original sin or capable of offering a utopian solution or substitute for the perfect society which Christ alone will establish at his Second Coming.

Article XI: War

We affirm that God desires peace and righteousness among nations and condemns wars of aggression.

We affirm that lawful states have the right and duty to defend their territories and citizens against aggression and oppression by other powers, including the provision for an adequate civil defense of the population.

We affirm that in rightful defense of their territories and citizens governments should only use just means of warfare.

We affirm that warring states should strive by every means possible to minimize civilian casualties.

We deny that the cause of Christ can be defended with earthly weapons.

We deny that Christians are forbidden to use weapons in the defense of lawful states.

We deny that the indiscriminate slaughter of civilians can be a moral form of warfare.

We deny that the circumstances of modern warfare destroy the right and duty of the civil government to defend its territories and citizens.

Article XII: Discrimination and Human Rights

We affirm that God, who created man and woman in his image, has granted to all human beings fundamental rights which are to be protected, sustained, and fostered on the natural and spiritual levels.

We affirm that all human beings are ultimately accountable to God for their use of these rights.

We affirm that Christians must uphold and defend the rights of others while being willing to relinquish their own rights for the good of others.

We affirm that Christians are admonished to follow the compassionate example of Jesus by helping to bear the burdens of those whose human rights have been diminished.

We deny that any so-called human right which violates the teaching of Scripture is legitimate.

We deny that any act is acceptable that would harm or diminish another person's natural or spiritual life by violating that person's human rights.

We deny that age, disability, economic disadvantage, race, religion, or sex used as a basis for discrimination can ever justify denial of the exercise or enjoyment of human rights.

We deny that elitism or grasping for power are compatible with Christ's call to dedicate our rights to his service.

Article XIII: Economics

We affirm that valid economic principles can be found in Scripture and should form an integral part of a Christian world and life view.

We affirm that material resources are a blessing from God, to be enjoyed with thanksgiving, and are to be earned, managed, and shared as a stewardship under God.

We affirm that Christians should give sacrificially of their resources to support the work of God's church.

We affirm that the use of personal and material resources for the proclamation of the gospel is necessary both for the salvation of lost mankind and to overcome poverty where that is fostered by adherence to non-Christian religious systems.

We affirm that active compassion for the poor and oppressed is an obligation that God places upon all human beings, especially on those with resources.

We affirm that the possession of wealth imposes obligations upon its possessors.

We affirm that the love of money is a source of great evil.

We affirm that human depravity, greed, and the will to power foster economic injustice and subvert concern for the poor.

We affirm that the Bible affirms the right of private ownership as a stewardship under God.

We deny that Scripture directly teaches any science of economics, although there are principles of economics that can be derived from Scripture.

We deny that Scripture teaches that compassion for the poor must be expressed exclusively through one particular economic system.

We deny that the Scripture teaches that money or wealth is inherently evil.

We deny that Scripture endorses economic collectivism or economic individualism.

We deny that Scripture forbids the use of capital resources to produce income.

We deny that the proper focus of a Christian's hope is material prosperity.

We deny that Christians should use their resources primarily for self-gratification.

We deny that salvation from sin necessarily involves economic or political liberation.

Article XIV: Work and Leisure

We affirm that God created humankind in his image and graciously fitted them for both work and leisure.

We affirm that in all honorable work, however menial, God works with and through the worker.

We affirm that work is the divinely ordained means whereby we glorify God and supply both our own needs and the needs of others.

We affirm that Christians should work to the best of their ability so as to please God.

We affirm that people should both humbly submit to and righteously exercise whatever authority operates in their sphere of work.

We affirm that in their work people should seek first God's kingdom and righteousness, depending on him to supply their material needs.

We affirm that compensation should be a fair return for the work done without discrimination.

We affirm that leisure, in proper balance with work, is ordained by God and should be enjoyed to his glory.

We affirm that work and its product have not only temporal but also eternal value when done and used for God's glory.

We deny that persons should pursue their work to fulfill and gratify themselves rather than to serve and please God.

We deny that the rich have more right to leisure than the poor.

We deny that certain types of work give persons greater value in God's eyes than other persons have.

We deny that the Christian should either depreciate leisure or make a goal of it.

Article XV: Wealth and Poverty

We affirm that God, who is just and loving, has a special concern for the poor in their plight.

We affirm that God calls for responsible stewardship by his people of both their lives and resources.

We affirm that sacrificial effort to relieve the poverty, oppression, and suffering of others is a hallmark of Christian discipleship.

We affirm that just as the wealthy ought not be greedy so the poor ought not to be covetous.

We deny that we may rightly call ourselves disciples of Christ if we lack active concern for the poor, oppressed, and suffering, especially those of the household of faith.

We deny that we may always regard prosperity or poverty as the measure of our faithfulness to Christ.

We deny that it is necessarily wrong for Christians to be wealthy or for some persons to possess more than others.

Article XVI: Stewardship of the Environment

We affirm that God created the physical environment for his own glory and for the good of his human creatures.

We affirm that God deputized humanity to govern the creation.

We affirm that mankind has more value than the rest of creation.

We affirm that mankind's dominion over the earth imposes a responsibility to protect and tend its life and resources.

We affirm that Christians should embrace responsible scientific investigation and its application in technology.

We affirm that stewardship of the Lord's earth includes the productive use of its resources which must always be replenished as far as possible.

We affirm that avoidable pollution of the earth, air, water, or space is irresponsible.

We deny that the cosmos is valueless apart from mankind.

We deny that the biblical view authorizes or encourages wasteful exploitation of nature.

We deny that Christians should embrace the countercultural repudiation of science or the mistaken belief that science is the hope of mankind.

We deny that individuals or societies should exploit the universe's resources for their own advantage at the expense of other people and societies.

We deny that a materialistic world view can provide an adequate basis for recognizing environmental values.

NOTES

Chapter 1 A Place to Stand

1. C. S. Lewis, *The Screwtape Letters* (New York: The Macmillan Company, 1943), p. 11.

2. News report by Dan Martin of the Baptist Press, Nashville, Tennessee.

3. Irenaeus, *Against Heresies*, II, xxvii, 2. *The Ante-Nicene Fathers*, vol. 1, ed. Alexander Roberts and James Donaldson (Grand Rapids: Wm. B. Eerdmans, n.d.), p. 399. Original edition 1885.

4. Cyril of Jerusalem, *Catechetical Lectures*, IV, 17. *The Nicene and Post-Nicene Fathers*, series 2, vol. 7, ed. Philip Schaff and Henry Wace (Grand Rapids: Wm. B. Eerdmans, n.d.), p. 23. Original edition 1893.

5. Augustine, "On the Trinity," Preface to ch. 3. *The Nicene and Post-Nicene Fathers*, series 1, vol. 3, ed. Philip Schaff (Grand Rapids: Wm. B. Eerdmans, 1978), p. 56. Original edition 1887.

6. Augustine, *Epistles*, 82. *The Fathers of the Church*, vol. 12, "St. Augustine: Letters 1–82," trans. Wilfrid Parsons (Washington, D.C.: The Catholic University of America Press, 1951), pp. 392, 409.

7. Martin Luther, "Preface to the Old Testament." *What Luther Says: An Anthology*, compiled by Ewald M. Plass, vol. 1 (Saint Louis: Concordia Publishing House, 1959), p. 71.

8. Martin Luther, "That Doctrines of Men Are to Be Rejected." Op. cit., p. 63.

9. Martin Luther, *Table Talk*, 44. *A Compend of Luther's Theology*, ed. Hugh Thompson Kerr (Philadelphia: The Westminster Press, 1943), p. 10.

10. John Calvin, *Calvin's Commentaries,* vol. 10, "The Second Epistle of Paul the Apostle to the Corinthians and the Epistles to Timothy, Titus and Philemon," trans. T. A. Smail (Grand Rapids: Wm. B. Eerdmans, 1964), p. 330.

11. John Wesley, *Journal,* Wednesday, July 24, 1776. *The Works of John Wesley,* vol. 4 (Grand Rapids: Zondervan Publishing House, n.d.), p. 82. Original edition 1872.

12. J. Gresham Machen, *The Attack Upon Princeton Seminary: A Plea for Fair Play* (Philadelphia: Johnson and Prince, 1927), p. 37.

13. R. A. Torrey, *The Bible and Its Christ* (New York: Fleming H. Revell, 1904–1906), p. 57.

14. Francis A. Schaeffer, "God Gives His People a Second Opportunity." *The Foundation of Biblical Authority,* ed. James Montgomery Boice (Grand Rapids: Zondervan Publishing House, 1978), p. 19.

15. J. I. Packer, *"Fundamentalism" and the Word of God* (Grand Rapids: Wm. B. Eerdmans, 1958), pp. 173, 174.

Chapter 2 The Way God Speaks

1. Martin Luther, "Only the Bible to Teach about God." *What Luther Says: An Anthology,* compiled by Ewald M. Plass, vol. 1 (Saint Louis: Concordia Publishing House, 1959), p. 81.

2. Benjamin Breckinridge Warfield, "The Biblical Idea of Inspiration." *The Inspiration and Authority of the Bible,* ed. Samuel G. Craig (Philadelphia: Presbyterian and Reformed, 1948), p. 133.

3. "A mighty wind . . . swept over the surface of the waters" (NEB).

4. James Montgomery Boice, *Does Inerrancy Matter?* (Wheaton: Tyndale House Publishers, 1981), p. 15. The wording was developed by the International Council on Biblical Inerrancy in its early days.

Chapter 3 Positive Evidence for the Bible

1. Benjamin Breckinridge Warfield, *The Inspiration and Authority of the Bible,* ed. Samuel G. Craig (Philadelphia: Presbyterian and Reformed, 1948). The volume contains nine major essays by Warfield spanning the years 1892–1915.

2. Cf. John Wenham, *Christ and the Bible* (Downers Grove, Ill.: InterVarsity Press, 1972).

3. Thomas Watson, *A Body of Divinity Contained in Sermons Upon the Westminster Assembly's Catechism* (London: The Banner of Truth Trust, 1958), p. 26. Original edition 1692.

4. R. A. Torrey, *The Bible and Its Christ* (New York: Fleming H. Revell, 1904–1906), p. 26.

5. F. F. Bruce, *The New Testament Documents: Are They Reliable?* (Downers Grove, Ill.: InterVarsity Press, 1974), p. 82.

6. E. Schuyler English, *A Companion to the New Scofield Reference Bible* (New York: Oxford University Press, 1972), p. 26.

7. H. A. Ironside, *Random Reminiscences from Fifty Years of Ministry* (New York: Loizeaux Brothers, 1939), pp. 99–107.

8. Portions of this chapter have appeared in a somewhat different form in James Montgomery Boice, *Foundations of the Christian Faith* (Downers Grove, Ill.: InterVarsity Press, 1986), pp. 37–66.

Chapter 4 Understanding God's Book

1. "The Canons and Dogmatic Decrees of the Council of Trent," Fourth Session, April 8, 1546. *The Creeds of Christendom with a History and Critical Notes*, ed. Philip Schaff, vol. 2 (New York: Harper & Brothers, 1877), p. 83.

2. E. C. Blackman, *Biblical Interpretation* (Philadelphia: The Westminster Press, 1957), p. 141.

3. Emil G. Kraeling, *The Old Testament Since the Reformation* (New York: Harper & Brothers, 1955), p. 94.

4. Rudolph Bultmann, *Jesus and the Word* (New York: Charles Scribner's Sons, 1934), p. 8.

5. R. C. Sproul, *Knowing Scripture* (Downers Grove, Ill.: InterVarsity Press, 1977), p. 37.

6. "The Westminster Confession of Faith" (1, IX). *The Creeds of Christendom with a History and Critical Notes*, ed. Philip Schaff, vol. 3 (New York: Harper & Brothers, 1877), p. 605.

7. See Appendix B.

8. Frank E. Gaebelein, *Exploring the Bible: A Study of Background and Principles* (Wheaton: Van Kampen Press, 1950), p. 134. Original edition 1929.

9. J. I. Packer, *"Fundamentalism" and the Word of God* (Grand Rapids: Wm. B. Eerdmans, 1958), p. 102.

10. Ibid., 102, 103.

11. Portions of this chapter have appeared in a somewhat different form in James Montgomery Boice, *Foundations of the Christian Faith* (Downers Grove, Ill.: InterVarsity Press, 1986), pp. 67–98, 492–499.

Chapter 5 Alleged Problems in the Bible

1. Harold Lindsell, *The Battle for the Bible* (Grand Rapids: Zondervan Publishing House, 1976), pp. 165, 166.

2. James B. Pritchard, editor, *Ancient Near Eastern Texts Relating to the Old Testament* (Princeton: Princeton University Press, 1955), p. 275.

3. *Time*, Dec. 30, 1974, p. 41.

4. *Time*, Jan. 13, 1975, p. 65.

5. William LaSor, "Life Under Tension—Fuller Theological Seminary and 'The Battle for the Bible.'" *The Authority of Scripture at Fuller* (Pasadena, Calif.: Fuller Theological Seminary, *Theology News and Notes*, Special Issue, 1976), pp. 5–10, 23–28.

6. Dewey M. Beegle, *Scripture, Tradition and Infallibility* (Grand Rapids: Wm. B. Eerdmans, 1973), pp. 175–197.

7. Gleason L. Archer, "Alleged Errors and Discrepancies in the Original Manuscripts of the Bible." Norman L. Geisler, editor, *Inerrancy* (Grand Rapids: Zondervan Publishing House, 1979), pp. 57–82.

8. J. Gresham Machen, *The Virgin Birth of Christ* (London: James Clarke, 1930), pp. 202–209.

9. Donald Grey Barnhouse, *Man's Ruin*, vol. 1 of the series on Romans (Grand Rapids: Wm. B. Eerdmans, 1952), pp. 45–47.

Chapter 6 The Most Useful Thing in the World

1. Charles W. Colson, "Foreword." J. I. Packer, *Freedom and Authority* (Oakland: International Council on Biblical Inerrancy, 1981), p. 3.

2. Jonathan Edwards, "Men Naturally Are God's Enemies." *The Works of Jonathan Edwards*, vol. 2 (Edinburgh and Carlisle, Pa.: The Banner of Truth Trust, 1976), pp. 130–141. Original edition 1834.

3. Emile Cailliet, *Journey Into Light* (Grand Rapids: Zondervan Publishing House, 1968), pp. 11–18.

Chapter 7 The Sufficiency of Scripture

1. Donald Grey Barnhouse, "Isaiah 55:11" in *Holding Forth the Word: 1927–1952* (Manuscript Collection of Tenth Presbyterian Church).

2. *Ibid.*

3. W. A. Criswell, "What Happens When I Preach the Bible as Literally True" in Earl D. Radmacher, editor, *Can We Trust the Bible?* (Wheaton: Tyndale House Publishers, 1979), pp. 91–108.

4. Marcellus Kik, *Church and State: The Story of Two Kingdoms* (New York: Thomas Nelson & Sons, 1963), p. 83. The full story of the changes brought about in Calvin's Geneva is told on pp. 71–85.

5. Donald Grey Barnhouse, "Faith and the Word" in *Epistle to the Romans*, part 62, *Romans 10:14–19* (Philadelphia: The Bible Study Hour, 1956), p. 32.